Jane Deverson

Know Your Personality

Futura Publications Limited

A Futura Book

First published in Great Britain by
Futura Publications Limited in 1980

Copyright © Jane Deverson 1980

ISBN 0 7088 1824 2
Typeset, printed and bound in Great Britain
by Hazell Watson & Viney Limited
Aylesbury, Bucks

Futura Publications Limited
110 Warner Road
Camberwell, London SE5

Contents

YOUR RELATIONSHIPS

Introduction

Relationships probably cause more happiness and more misery than anything else in life. Our needs seem very simple—basically to love and be loved; to appreciate other people and to be appreciated ourselves. These seemingly simple needs easily become lost, hidden, denied and distorted in the innumerable complications of human relationships.

It is often difficult to know exactly what you want from people, and to know what they expect of *you*; it is difficult to see yourself as other people see you; it is difficult to understand how your own behaviour influences other people's reactions to you and their treatment of you; how your own personality and your own emotions determine the course of your relationships.

I hope you enjoy participating in this self-analysis quiz book. I hope it will help you to realize more about your motives and desires, and to gain more insight into your relationships.

Jane Deverson

PEOPLE AND PLACES QUIZ

Look at the incomplete pictures devoid of human content. Imagining you are the artist, choose the people you would put into each scene. Just be guided by your own feelings and instincts about each picture.

1. *The Village Green*

    (a) A few old people around the edge of the green, some children playing, dogs scampering about.
    (b) The village parson in his surplice walking across the green.
    (c) A fairground scene in the middle of the green.

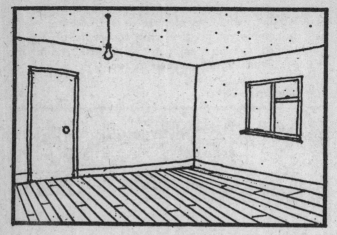

(a) A rather surrealist atmosphere, leave room as it is, with man in suit sitting alone cross-legged in middle of floor.

(b) Give the room 1930s *décor*, who-dunnit scene with dead girl on sofa, trilby-hatted detectives, etc.

(c) Give the room Victorian furniture, parlour scene with typical Victorian family.

(a) A couple at the bus stop, a group of teenagers on opposite pavement and a woman with shopping bags crossing the road.

(b) An old woman and a schoolboy awaiting at the bus stop.

(c) A couple waiting at the bus stop, a cyclist on the road and a man walking along the pavement opposite.

(a) Bird-creatures with women's heads, flowing hair and huge, feathered wings.

(b) Beautiful nymph children in foreground, playing musical instruments.

(c) Demon-like figures dancing and breathing out fire.

5. *Country Landscape*

(a) Include some farm animals and some men working in the fields.

(b) A hunting scene with hounds and people on
horses chasing across the landscape.

(c) Include a small figure of a shepherd with his dog
on one of the foothills.

6. *Bus Interior*

(a) Three or four people, each a portrait, dotted over the seats of the bus at artistic intervals to make a good composition.

(b) Every seat filled, a scene of lots of people, some talking, some silent, some happy, some sad-looking, etc.

(c) Empty apart from the back seat where a couple of lovers sit with their arms round each other.

Marshland Scene

(a) A group of Romany-looking gypsies and their encampment.
(b) It is an intrinsically atmospheric landscape—no people would be included.
(c) Several parachutists dropping from the sky with spectators watching from the ground.

(a) An old tramp by the side of the road.
(b) A couple looking happy and exhilarated, wind-blown, in an open-roofed car.
(c) A fleet of teenagers on motorbikes, obviously speeding and racing each other.

English Country Garden

(a) Close-up portrait of young girl with basket of flowers, the garden as a background.

(b) A garden-party scene with people milling about, drinking, talking, etc.

(c) Just a gothic-looking stone statue of a woman in the middle distance.

(a) Panic scene with people running for safety.
(b) One person running for safety, a few dead bodies strewn about.
(c) A group of people watching in awe from the safety of the rocks in the foreground.

See SCORING PAGE.

SCORING PAGE
Scoring Key

1. The Village Green
   (a) = 2 Points   (b) = 3   (c) = 1
2. Room Interior
   (a) = 3 Points   (b) = 1   (c) = 2
3. Suburban Street
   (a) = 1 Point   (b) = 3   (c) = 2
4. Fantasia
   (a) = 3 Points   (b) = 2   (c) = 1
5. Country Landscape
   (a) = 2 Points   (b) = 1   (c) = 3
6. Bus Interior
   (a) = 3 Points   (b) = 1   (c) = 2
7. Marshland Scene
   (a) = 2 Points   (b) = 3   (c) = 1
8. Modern-Art Motorway
   (a) = 3 Points   (b) = 2   (c) = 1
9. English Country Garden
   (a) = 2 Points   (b) = 1   (c) = 3
10. Disaster Scene
    (a) = 1 Point   (b) = 3   (c) = 2

Enter your score here and total:

1. ☐   5. ☐   8. ☐
2. ☐   6. ☐   9. ☐
3. ☐   7. ☐   10. ☐
4. ☐

Total.............

10–16 Points—See CONCLUSION ONE.
17–23 Points—See CONCLUSION TWO.
24–30 Points—See CONCLUSION THREE.

CONCLUSION ONE

You want to fill your world with people, the more the merrier. You are attracted to crowds. You need the excitement and stimulation of a lot of people around you, and you enjoy the feeling of being at the centre of the activity.

Being naturally gregarious your ideal social environment must give you scope for new contacts and novel situations, and for this reason you are probably happier living in the city than the country. You will tend to gravitate towards centres of entertainment and places where people congregate.

Your identity is very much bound up with other people, and you see yourself as part of the wider social scene. You genuinely like *people*, not just as individuals, but as members of the human race. You have a great desire to communicate with them and to become involved with them. You look for entertainment and sensation, but you also need a constant response from others, and emotional feedback from them, and you may even lose a sense of reality if you are on your own for too long because people are so much a part of your life, and your identity.

You can often gauge your happiness by the extent of your social life; your feeling of well-being by the warmth and frequency of your encounters with friends and acquaintances. So the more easily you can make friends and the more you are included in social events, the happier you are likely to be.

You are good at fitting into different environments and adapting to different types of person. You do not always look for soul-mates, but can be attracted to opposites and intrigued by other people's differences.

You find it easy to meld into different life-styles; for you do not need to feel you are in control of your environment, but can usually accept it for what it is. In fact you are often most excited and stimulated when events are out of your direct control and sensation can take over. You find great pleasure in throwing yourself into situations, be-

20

ing socially adventurous, catching the spirit of the occasion and being swept along by the atmosphere of the crowd or group of the moment.

Your search for sensation can take many forms. In some cases it will be a search for sexual adventures with a variety of people, a tendency to drink too much and generally overdo the wilder side of your social life. In other cases it will be a more generalized search for fun and enjoyment, and in other cases perhaps a desire to participate in some thrilling or dangerous sport or hobby—anything from skin-diving to hang-gliding, for instance.

In your social life generally you need new opportunities and a sense of variety. It is likely that when a social pattern becomes predictable and there are no opportunities for sexual excitement, you will lose interest and look for a change.

You don't always want or need deep relationships with people. People may sometimes quickly lose their novelty value in which case you will become restless and bored. At the best you enjoy social life on an impulsive, easy-going level; mixing with others for the mutual stimulation and enjoyment you get out of it.

People are a genuine therapy for you and in the company of others you find a release from tension and anxiety, you find the emotional warmth you thrive on, the fulfilment of giving your personality and receiving friendship and the expression of other people's personalities in return. The need for human contact, on whatever level, is a very real and important motivation in your life, and if it is not at least partially satisfied you cannot be happy.

CONCLUSION TWO

You want to fill your world with people who are close to you and familiar to you, and you look for deeply emotional and personal contacts with people.

Ideally your social environment should be large enough to allow for variety, but also small enough to give you a feeling of community spirit and togetherness with others. You look for a sense of belonging, and you want to be automatically accepted in a friendly circle of people. You need the security of being welcomed without question, and for this reason you would be happy in a 'village' atmosphere, whether the 'village' is in the country, in a block of flats or housing estate, or a small corner of a town or suburb where people know and care about each other. Being attracted to close-knit groups, you would probably enjoy belonging to a club, being a member of a committee or action group, or just building up an informal social group which meets regularly in a place of entertainment or each other's homes.

Your environment is important to you because you associate places with people, and it is likely that you become attached to places if the atmosphere is right. Once you have found somewhere where you feel at home—an environment which caters for the needs of your personality—you will probably be happy to stay there and put down roots.

You identify closely with people around you and become deeply involved with them. Generally the more you get to know people the more you like them. Although you are sociable and you probably enjoy meeting new people, you are basically happier with friends than with acquaintances.

You are sensitive to the social climate around you and your moods and feelings are affected by the people you mix with. You become concerned with *their* concerns, you become happy or sad for them and you find it easy to tune into their emotions. You need other people and you want to be needed by them.

Basically you enjoy co-operating with people, building up trust, affection and sympathy and working towards harmony in your relationship and your immediate environment. If you really feel you belong to a group or a community you will identify very strongly with it, and there will be a sense of purpose as well as pleasure in your social life. You want to be able to feel that you are building up towards common aims and goals, and your personal ambitions will not be very satisfying to you unless you can share them with people around you.

You need real friendship and approval. Too much chaos will be disturbing to you, even though you may welcome a certain amount of excitement and diversion from routine. A feeling of isolation, of rejection or being excluded from the warmth and reassurance of the group will be unbearable to you. Perhaps soullessness and indifference are worst of all—you look for a deeply emotional response, for the loyalty of the group, and for genuine and lasting commitment in your close relationships.

Ideally you need to achieve a balance between the stimulation of new contacts and experience and the background of peace and security among people you know, love and trust.

CONCLUSION THREE

You do not always need or want to fill your world with people. Being an introverted person with a high level of internal control, you can be alone without feeling isolated, you can value your own company and enjoy being the centre of your own world.

You tend to see yourself as a separate person, without necessarily putting yourself into a social setting, so even though you may have good friends and a satisfying social life you still have a strong sense of being yourself rather than incorporating your identity into the group. You don't have an automatic fellow-feeling for others, and people for the sake of people have little interest for you. You probably dislike crowds and become nervous or irritated when too many strangers are too close to you. Your instinct will be to back away and seek solitude.

Very often you will have difficulty in relating to people around you; you will not naturally sympathize with their

23

goals and aims in life, and you will not easily become emotionally involved with them simply because of their physical proximity, because they happen to be neighbours or working colleagues, etc. So you will sometimes feel detached from your surroundings, lacking a sense of community and belonging, observing the scene around you rather than participating actively in it.

Although you tend to stand on the outside of social groups, you appreciate people as individuals and close relationships are highly valued and extremely important to you. You are willing to give your friendship for life and a friend gained will seldom be lost.

In keeping with your individual approach your relationships are not likely to run to a pattern—your friends will be chosen for their individual qualities and for the particular emotional bond between you. Friendship is a serious and enjoyable commitment which can span years and physical distance—for instance, old friends who are seldom seen are not forgotten and your fond feelings for people are not likely to change or even to fade very much with time.

In general even if you belong to a social group you won't let it anchor you, influence you too much or take over too much of you. Your environment as such is not very important to you—you will be the same person wherever you go, and it is unlikely that you will become attached to places.

Relationships are not always a motivating force in your life, in fact your search for self-fulfilment may be more important to you than relationships, and loneliness is something you often have to come to terms with. You want to be yourself, and you are not happy to make too many concessions to those around you.

You search for a unique experience of life. If people and social scenes fit in with your personality and your aims you will align yourself to them. If not you may isolate yourself and go your own way.

A love match depends for its success on the blending of your personality with someone else's, on the qualities in your partner which are in sympathy or complementary to your qualities, and on both your abilities to gratify each other's needs.

If you understand your own personality and you are aware of your own needs it is much easier to make a wise decision in choosing someone you can be happy with. There is no ideal type as such, because different people will appeal to different aspects of your personality, but it is still possible to make a reasonably accurate prediction about the types you will find it easiest to blend with, and the kind of relationship which is likely to develop with different types of people.

The Matchmaker Quiz is firstly a personality test to give an outline of your character. You will fall into one of the six basic types. After you have read the Personality Conclusions turn to the Matchmaker Combinations to find out how you are likely to get on with your own type, and with the five other types categorized in the quiz.

In each set of two statements tick the one which applies most to you. If you feel neither are particularly characteristic of you still do your best to pick the nearest approximation.

Be as honest as possible in your choices, disregarding any 'good/bad', socially acceptable/unacceptable implications you may read into the statements.

1. (a) Loneliness/discontent have the effect of making you withdraw from society.
   (b) Loneliness/discontent have the effect of driving you into action in society.
2. (a) You tend not to put enough effort into casual relationships in general.
   (b) You tend not to put enough effort into close relationships.

3. (a) When you are ill at ease with someone you have just met you tend to talk too little.
   (b) When you are ill at ease with someone you have just met you tend to talk too much.

4. (a) You suffer most from sadness/gloom/despondency.
   (b) You suffer most from boredom/irritation/restlessness.

5. (a) You tend to be shy or reserved when you first meet people.
   (b) You enjoy first encounters with comparative ease.

6. (a) You can enjoy experiences in solitude.
   (b) Usually you can only enjoy experiences if they are shared with someone else.

7. (a) You tend only to get on with people who are on your wavelength.
   (b) You can get on with most people, at least on the surface.

8. (a) You are a thoughtful person.
   (b) You are an active person.

9. (a) You tend to wait for people to come to you.
   (b) You tend to seek people out.

10. (a) You feel irritated and/or threatened in a large crowd.
    (b) You find it quite exciting or at least non-threatening to be in a large crowd.

11. (a) Certain types of people often make you nervous.
    (b) Certain types of people often make you angry.

12. (a) You need to spend time thinking/day-dreaming about personal joys and problems.
    (b) You don't often feel the need for private thinking/day-dreaming time.

13. (a) Your relationships must be either on an emotional or mentally stimulating level to be enjoyable.
    (b) You can enjoy relationships on different levels.

14. (a) You are most likely to feel self-conscious and embarrassed in a group.
    (b) You are most likely to feel a competitive urge to assert yourself in a group.

15. (a) Your general tendency is to seek perfection.
    (b) You tend to make the best of what is there.

16. (a) You are generally rather cautious.
    (b) You can cope with and even enjoy an element of risk.

17. (a) You are inclined to put on a display of modesty when complimented and praised.
    (b) You show your pleasure openly when complimented and praised.

18. (a) You feel people find you more and more interesting/likeable, etc. the more they get to know you.
    (b) You feel you make an immediate impression, that people see your good qualities almost at once.

19. (a) You would choose loneliness rather than mixing with people you don't like.
    (b) You would probably mix with people you don't like rather than be lonely.

20. (a) You are careful not to cause hurt or embarrassment to people.
    (b) You reckon most people can take a fair amount of ribbing/criticism.

21. (a) You sometimes find yourself 'lost' in thought even when you are part of a social gathering.
    (b) You give the occasion your full attention when you are part of a social gathering.

Mostly (a)—Go on to SECTION A.
Mostly (b)—Go on to SECTION B.

1. Do you find you are mostly attracted towards—
    (a) rather glamorous people?
    (c) rather clever or witty, unusual people?
    (b) rather powerful, self-confident people?

2. What is your reaction to explosive, irrational, emotional scenes and quarrels?
    (c) You have no patience for them, finding them irritating and unpleasant.
    (b) You dislike them, and become hurt, upset and depressed by them.
    (a) You rather enjoy them sometimes, actually.

3. How do you feel at the prospect of going on a social outing or to a party on your own?
    (b) You'd feel rather diminished and apprehensive without a partner.
    (a) You'd feel excited, wondering what impression you will make and whom you will meet, etc.
    (c) You'd quite enjoy going on your own, but without any particular fear or excitement.

4. At the beginning of a very promising relationship, are you most inclined to—
    (a) fantasize in quite elaborate detail on the way you'd like the relationship to progress?
    (c) analyze the relationship as extensively and accurately as you can?
    (b) become mainly preoccupied in wondering whether and hoping that the other person feels as strongly about you and you do about them?

5. Which seems most important to you in a relationship?
    (c) Communication of interests, thoughts and ideas.
    (b) Emotional closeness and understanding.
    (a) A kind of 'magical' quality.

6. What do you dislike about your image of typical Suburbia?
    (b) The soulless quality of no real community, no sense of belonging.

(a) The dreariness, routine and lack of variety.

(c) The emphasis on materialistic things, limited mental horizons.

7. In non-sexual friendships and friendships with the same sex, do you—

(a) Become bored with the same friend for too long and feel the need for fresh company?

(c) Become bored with too much of the same friend and feel the need for privacy?

(b) Feel able to tolerate closeness with one friend for unlimited time?

8. Which of the following statements is most true of you?

(c) You make plans for the future, build up towards ambitions and take stock of your situation from time to time.

(b) You tend to drift rather and fall in with other people's arrangements, even though you may have ambitions of your own.

(a) You tend to have rather high-flown aspirations in life, without a very clear idea of how you are going to carry them out.

9. Which of the following would be most essential to you in a long-term relationship?

(b) Making each other feel loved and needed.

(c) Respecting each other's individuality.

(a) Keeping each other stimulated and fascinated.

10. If your partner or a close friend developed views and attitudes totally opposed to your own, how would you react?

(c) You would accept the fact, and your basic feelings for them wouldn't change.

(a) You would find it intolerable, either losing respect for them or constantly trying to convert them back.

(b) You would adapt to their view, try to understand and even perhaps adopt the same attitudes, especially if you love and/or admire the other person.

Mostly (a)—Read CONCLUSION ONE—
         then turn to the MATCHMAKER
         COMBINATIONS.
Mostly (b)—Read CONCLUSION TWO—
         then MATCHMAKER
         COMBINATIONS.
Mostly (c)—Read CONCLUSION THREE—
         then MATCHMAKER
         COMBINATIONS.

SECTION B

1. Do you usually find very close, exclusive relationships with one person—
   (a) very satisfying?
   (c) a bit restricting?
   (b) rather boring after a while?

2. Seeing a stranger whom you find very attractive, do
   you find yourself wondering mostly—
   (c) about their background, job, general life-style
       and status in life?
   (a) what their character is like, how they think and
       feel?
   (b) what sort of social and love life they have?

3. Which is nearest to your reaction when a partner/
   friend goes through quite a serious bout of depression or illness?
   (a) You are sympathetic and can remain patient,
       pleased to help, comfort, give moral support.
   (b) You try to be sympathetic, but you can't help
       finding them tedious and unlovable somehow.
   (c) You try to be sympathetic, but you can't help
       despising their weakness to some extent, and re-
       senting them a bit.

4. Do your private thoughts and day-dreams tend to
   revolve mostly around—
   (b) sexual pleasures and excesses?
   (c) heights of ambition and achievement?

(a) practical planning and day-dreams based on reality?

5. What is your instinct when someone you don't know very well (say at work or in public) is hostile or verbally abusive to you without warning—
  (c) immediate counter-attack, matching their hostility or outdoing it?
  (b) refusal to take it very seriously, making light of it?
  (a) keep control but level with them firmly, demand an explanation?

6. How would you feel about having your ancestry and family history traced back?
  (b) You wouldn't bother.
  (a) You'd be quite interested.
  (c) You'd be fascinated.

7. Would it give you the most pleasure to be complimented on—
  (a) your strength of character?
  (c) your forceful personality?
  (b) your charm and popularity?

8. In a business deal or arrangement do you think you'd be inclined to—
  (c) drive a hard bargain?
  (b) be easy-going and probably on the generous side?
  (a) weigh things up quite carefully in an effort to be fair?

9. How important is physical attractiveness to you in a long-term or casual relationship with the opposite sex?
  (b) Essential—you couldn't really enjoy a relationship unless you found the other person extremely handsome/beautiful.
  (a) You like attractive people, but if you fell in love with someone a bit plain it wouldn't matter.
  (c) It's important socially—you would feel slightly

31

ashamed of being with someone who wasn't attractive in the eyes of the world.

10. How do you react to periods of conflict, tension, rows, emotional upsets with your partner?

(a) You try to take control of the situation and make the other person see reason.

(c) Your behaviour tends to become rather extreme—noisy scenes, bitter arguments and accusations, loss of temper, perhaps physical violence in some form.

(b) You tend to react by detaching yourself emotionally, trying to find solace, friendship and satisfaction elsewhere.

Mostly (a)—Read CONCLUSION FOUR—
then turn to the MATCHMAKER
COMBINATIONS.

Mostly (b)—Read CONCLUSION FIVE—
then MATCHMAKER
COMBINATIONS.

Mostly (c)—Read CONCLUSION SIX—
then MATCHMAKER
COMBINATIONS.

CONCLUSION ONE—ROMANTIC

You are an emotional idealist, seeking heights of feeling and unusual experiences, often with a rather spiritual 'larger than life' quality. Craving for perfection in your relationships, you find it difficult to come to terms with people's faults or to make allowances. But even though you know life is seldom as wonderful as you would like it to be, you still get a lot of pleasure and satisfaction from your romantic ideals.

You enjoy your inner perceptions and the sensitivity of your feelings, and you are happiest in an environment where you can express your inner personality, and where others will understand your wavelength and share your dreams. As you are rather introverted, you may sometimes find it difficult to communicate with people as much as you would like.

As a rule you dislike routine and detail. You act on your intuitions, and your judgements of others are based on instinct rather than logical reasoning.

There is likely to be a fairly wide gap between the kind of life you wish for, and your life in reality; but the fact that you often feel disappointed enables you to gain intense pleasure from the moments in life which really *do* live up to your expectations. A feeling of hopeful excitement runs through your life, and you tend to value all your experiences, both the good and the bad.

You may be able to adjust well to your life and to cope with restrictions and compromises, but you are never likely to lose your illusions and fantasies, your search for special emotional awareness, and your desire to be and to feel extraordinary in some respect.

CONCLUSION TWO—TENDER-HEARTED

You are emotional and tender-hearted, looking for close relationships with others. Your feelings for people tend to be persistent and enduring, so that once you decide you like someone, your feelings for them are likely to deepen

33

with time. You are sentimental and nostalgic about old friends, and a sense of real trust and loyalty is essential to you in all close relationships.

You are warm-hearted and kind. You have a great deal of genuine sympathy for others and can be moved to joy or unhappiness on their account. You are perceptive about the feelings of other people, with a sensitive awareness of subtle changes of mood and atmosphere.

Being introverted, you are often diffident about starting new relationships, needing time to get to know people quite well before you can feel at ease with them. So you tend to dislike fleeting, superficial relationships and social life which is too competitive in the sense of people putting on an act to impress each other.

Although you often appear to be tranquil and relaxed, you are prone to patches of moodiness and depression, and you worry quite a lot about your relationships. You are deeply affected by any sign of hostility or rejection and you need security and the reassurance that you are loved. You tend to be rather dependent on your partner. You enjoy the feeling of being protected up to a point, of having a strong ally to share all the emotional responsibilities which you take so seriously.

Your emotional reaction to life means that although you have your share of suffering, you are also capable of gaining great rewards and satisfactions from your relationships.

CONCLUSION THREE—INDEPENDENT

You are logical, tending to make intellectual rather than emotional judgements and decisions. Although you are theoretically tolerant, you tend to be critical in individual relationships, and you are extremely exacting in your expectations of friends and lovers.

You can afford to be fussy because you do not have a desperate need to align yourself with another person. You are independent enough to remain solitary until you can find the friendships you desire.

Generally you look for an intellectual equal, for someone who places a high value on communication, with a love of knowledge, learning and original thought.

You tend to hold your emotions back and to shy away from too many emotional demands. You need freedom to be yourself in a relationship, and your own sense of individuality often makes it difficult for you to merge with someone else. Although close relationships are extremely important to you, your personal integrity will prevent you from compromising, and this will sometimes be interpreted by others as coldness and lack of sympathy.

In social life generally you probably dislike small-talk, and you will seldom make the effort to be socially charming or to join in simply for the sake of bonhomie and popularity.

You are capable of mature relationships in which you can leave the other person alone sometimes, being willing to give them equal freedom and individuality, not asking for too much moral or emotional support, and not expecting the other person to demand too much from you, either. So although you are capable of giving loyalty and emotional understanding, there are areas of your life and your personality which you do not want to share, and you feel uneasy and irritated if the other person invades too much of your privacy.

CONCLUSION FOUR—REALISTIC

You have a 'big', generous personality, willing to face others on equal terms without any sense of pettiness or point-scoring. You are self-confident, realistic and mature in your approach to relationships. Although you don't generally make a display of your emotions, you understand the feelings of others and, when you feel that people deserve it, you go to a lot of trouble to be kind and protective.

You have your own personal sense of morality and justice, and although you are basically sympathetic to others, your judgements can be hard sometimes. Because you are a strong and courageous person, you sometimes find it difficult to condone weakness and cowardice, especially when you feel that the other person is not making enough effort to overcome his/her problems.

You normally look for practical solutions and you are very much in control of your emotions and of events and situations surrounding you. You have a natural inclination to be rather authoritarian, to organize people and take charge of situations. You enjoy being in a position where others trust your judgements and rely on you, and where your strength and your ability to cope are recognized. You are good at taking on responsibility for other people, and you have the gift of making them feel loved and secure.

Being an extrovert, you get on well with people and make friends easily, though not always on a deeply emotional level. You are generally extremely confident in close relationships. Having a strongly favourable image of yourself, you seldom suffer from self-doubt and you don't often have to question the fact that you are loved and needed. Your realistic approach helps you to enjoy relationships for what they are, without craving for romantic excesses or feeling too dissatisfied about limitations.

CONCLUSION FIVE—PLEASURE-SEEKING

You are optimistic and fun-loving, living for the pleasure of the moment, and having a facility for finding enjoyment in your environment more or less anywhere you happen to be. You are highly motivated towards sex and sensual pleasure. This is not usually a desperate need, but an inclination to gratify your desires whenever you can, and apart from gaining satisfaction for yourself, you also enjoy making other people happy.

You are extrovert and gregarious, extremely generous and warm-hearted. You enjoy money and material possessions simply for the fun to be gained from them. So you would be more likely to squander your money than to save it for security, or to see it as a status symbol.

You look for variety in your relationships and you often find it hard to centre your affections on one person. You are easily attracted to people, often instantly swayed emotionally, though the emotions are likely to be passionately explosive and short-lived. So long-term relationships tend to be a problem, especially with a possessive partner. You don't suffer very much from jealousy, and you find the trait difficult to understand and to put up with in others.

You are certainly a very kind person, very willing to see the good in people and to dismiss the bad, but most difficulties in your close relationships result from thoughtlessness. You are inclined to be impatient with inner emotional problems and in your urge for stimulation and variety you may not have time to stop and analyze relationships.

Your emotions are spontaneous and instinctive, your interests are many and diffused, and your social life tends to be hectic. In general you are a joyful person; you really appreciate your life and your happy moments; you genuinely like people, and there is a sincere warmth in your friendships.

CONCLUSION SIX—DYNAMIC
Your dynamic personality is liable to make enemies as well as friends, for you are sometimes tempted to assert yourself and get your own way at the expense of other people's wishes or feelings. You are lively minded and energetic, strongly motivated towards success, not only in achieving your personal objectives, but also in proving yourself to others.

You feel you have a wide audience to impress, so it is sometimes difficult to narrow your interests down to one person. Passionate and loving though you can be, your personal ambitions tend to override your relationships.

37

You are quixotic and highly responsive to your surroundings. You need stimulation and variety and you enjoy challenge and a certain amount of risk. You will aim high rather than building up step by step. You enjoy the kudos of being given responsibility but you are often too impatient to see responsibilities through to the ultimate conclusion.

In close relationships you are often unpredictable and demanding with a tendency to be egotistical, but at the same time you have great generosity of spirit and a willingness to share your enthusiasms and the good things of your life with the other person. You tend to become aggressive only when the other person tries to 'manage' you and restrict you.

You are socially extroverted and look for a wide range of friends and interests. Your emotions are sparked very easily. Although you can enjoy pleasant, aimless friendships up to a point, you prefer relationships to have a positive result—e.g. work-mates who can influence your career, people you can learn from and gain stimulation and ideas, etc.

MATCHMAKER COMBINATIONS
How you are likely to get on with someone who is the same type as you are—

Romantic and Romantic
This is likely to be an ecstatic relationship at the beginning; for you are able to make each other's fantasies and desires come true. This is the kind of love affair romantic fiction is made of. You both have the ability to enjoy the magical element of romance and to become swept away with emotion, so the relationship is a beautiful experience and you can both become totally obsessed and involved in it.

The trouble is, in the long term, that neither of you is very good at coping with the dreary aspects of reality, and your love may fade when life becomes humdrum or difficult. Emotional passion is hard to maintain at the level you would like when you begin to see each other as ordinary human beings with human faults. In this case you are likely to blame each other for the disillusionment, rather than helping each other to come to terms with it.

However, if you can keep the emotional glitter alive, perhaps by maintaining a glamorous or unusual life-style, then this could be a very rewarding relationship.

Alternatively you may realize that there is enough real feeling and affection between you to make the relationship worthwhile despite the loss of romantic excitement.

Tender-hearted and Tender-hearted

You are two of a kind and you recognize each other's need for a close, emotional relationship. You are loyal and sympathetic to each other, with a sensitive understanding of each other's feelings. At the beginning at least you feel you have found a soul-mate with an almost telepathic union between you. You will be deeply involved, and you enjoy the intense seriousness of the relationship. The relationship is built on loving kindness, consideration and trust, but perhaps in such a serious merging of emotions there is not enough outlet for fun and light-heartedness—in other words you may find the relationship becoming rather 'heavy'.

After a while you may realize that you are *too* similar. For instance, if your moods are too much in parallel you cannot provide much relief for each other, so that rather than one person helping the other out of a depression, you would be liable to sink into gloom together.

In the long term you would perhaps lack verve and vitality, as you would tend to limit each other to the familiar rather than introducing adventure and variety into the relationship. Another problem is likely to be that you find it difficult to help each other to maintain a lively social life, both being introverted and taking time to make friends.

The success of the relationship would depend on how much effort you both made to be more out-going, and how far you would continue to appreciate the quality of close, peaceful love and companionship.

Independent and Independent
This is a very good mature relationship in the modern sense, where each partner recognizes the other's right to freedom and self-expression, and neither of you attempts to restrict the other, or to impose rules and regulations.

You appreciate each other's interests and activities, and share them when you both feel inclined. The relationship is intellectually interesting and both of you feel you can develop your own personality, knowing that the other person won't resent you for it.

You can be genuine friends as well as lovers, because there is no question of ownership. You trust each other to be honourable, and the lack of emotional demands means that there is seldom cause for conflict or for the building up of hostilities.

If you are both as truly independent as you think you are, you will enjoy the freedom and mutual respect and tolerance of this relationship, as long as you don't become so separate that you no longer have any need for each other.

This kind of adult and mature relationship works very well as long as you can cope with it, but there is a possibility of neglecting each other's emotional needs, so that cold reasoning takes over. If you overdo the independence and self-sufficiency it's likely that one or both of you will begin to crave for more warmth and emotion.

Realistic and Realistic
This is a union of equals, two strong personalities together, with a mature attitude towards the relationship. You have goals and interests in common and you work well in partnership, building up towards mutual ambitions. You are both willing to work hard and to put a great

deal of effort into joint aims, so that you are likely to be a very successful couple in a long-term relationship—not just successful in the relationship itself, but also in the eyes of the world.

You have a basic respect for each other and you can also accept each other's imperfections. Conflict may arise because you both want to make the decisions, to cope with situations and be the controlling influence. So if both of you can agree to share responsibility rather than vying for control, you will have a very smooth-running and secure relationship. As you both have a strongly developed protective instinct, marriage and family life would be very satisfying. You are also able to enjoy social life together, both of you being extroverted and good at mixing with people.

The possible danger is that you will use all your energies on practical things and good management, forgetting how to communicate on an emotional level. You will have to guard against the relationship becoming too work-a-day and so realistic that there is no room for enough fantasy, imagination and emotional fulfilment.

Pleasure-seeking and Pleasure-seeking
Certainly this is a wonderful relationship to begin with. You have the same need for sexual adventure, sensual pleasure and material comfort, and you can cater for each other's needs without restraint or inhibition. There will be little tension, jealousy or guilt to spoil the fun, and you can be good friends as well as good lovers. You share the same optimism and enthusiasm for life, and you are both tireless in your enjoyment of the social scene.

You are tolerant and easy-going and so long as the attraction lasts this will be a genuinely loving relationship. However, it may lack emotional depth, with so much emphasis on the pursuit of pleasure and so much energy directed towards the external world rather than towards inner feelings.

In the longer term the problem might be that your joint life-style becomes too chaotic and unstable to be workable, as there will be no calming or restraining influence and neither of you excel at order or control.

Another likely problem will be to guard against boredom and disillusionment in the event of the excitement fading. A certain amount of tedium and routine is inevitable in all relationships and it's possible that you both lack stamina and understanding when the other partner fails to meet your expectations.

The danger is that when the intensive zest and attraction wears off you may find there is not very much left to replace it. The relationship will have a good chance of lasting happily if you can communicate on an emotional level and maintain your affection for each other, and your sense of humour.

Dynamic and Dynamic

This is an exciting, explosive relationship, full of the passion and drama which is so stimulating and satisfying to both of you. The jealousies, accusations and emotional scenes are all part of the fun. You enjoy releasing emotion on each other, and you enjoy the heightened passion and tenderness of making up after a fight.

As a couple you will be admired, perhaps even envied by your friends. The world is fascinated by you, especially if you are both young and beautiful, and you can both give each other the applause and admiration you seek. Your feelings for each other are genuine, even though surface emotions tend to be exaggerated.

In the long term the danger of two dynamic personalities together is that rather than boosting each other's egos you are likely to start competing to be the most powerful/attractive/popular partner of the relationship. This may start as a game in semi-seriousness, but once it becomes a habit the fighting is liable to become very bitter indeed, with resentment and hostility getting out of hand. You are both inclined to be egotistical, selfishly demanding, quick to take offence and to react violently, so there is a danger of ending up as real enemies.

The relationship can work well, firstly if both your energies and abilities are being used to the full in the relationship and outside it, and secondly if you can learn to tone down, to compromise and give and take.

How you are likely to get on with the other five types in the MATCHMAKER COMBINATIONS—

Romantic and Tender-hearted
You have a lot in common and you are attracted by your similarity of qualities. You are on the same wavelength and have an intuitive understanding of each other's feelings. The ROMANTIC person brings imagination, style and emotional expressiveness into the relationship, while the TENDER-HEARTED person responds with affection and emotional depths of feeling. You both look for emotional satisfaction and you are both day-dreamers who idealize love and seek a perfect relationship. Although your feelings for each other are very intense at first, there is a possibility of passions fading. At this stage more effort will have to be put into the relationship. The ROMANTIC partner may feel disappointed and discontented because the TENDER-HEARTED partner is not glamorous enough and fails to live up to the romantic ideal. The TENDER-HEARTED partner may begin to feel that the ROMANTIC partner is emotionally shallow and unpredictable, failing to provide real loving care and emotional security.

If these pitfalls can be avoided, this could be a happy, long-term relationship, the romantic gloss being replaced by sensitivity to each other's needs and a feeling of emotional closeness. There is likely to be an element of sentiment and nostalgia in the relationship, as you both value and wish to remember past experiences. The TENDER-

HEARTED partner will have to make allowances for the ROMANTIC's restlessness and need for variety, and the ROMANTIC partner should make allowances for the TENDER-HEARTED's need for closeness and belonging, and also for his or her bouts of silent brooding.

Independent and Realistic
You are both individuals with your own abilities and strengths, so this is a relationship of equals where you respect and appreciate each other's qualities. Although many of your attitudes and interests are likely to be different, your aims in life can merge, and you are good at planning the future together.

The REALISTIC partner sees the practical aspects of things, and the INDEPENDENT partner is more consciously analytical and concerned with theory, so you can both be helpful to each other, and you can both learn a lot from each other.

Though the REALIST is extroverted and the INDEPENDENT is an introvert, you can still enjoy social life together. You both have a mature attitude towards love and sex, and there are likely to be very few jealousies or emotional conflicts. If this is a married relationship it is likely that the sexual roles are not clearly defined, for you are both liberated in your approach to relationships.

If the REALISTIC person has a strong protective instinct he or she may be tempted to manage and control the relationship, and the INDEPENDENT person will resent this. There is a danger that the REALISTIC person will lack the feeling of being needed, and begin to feel emotionally isolated. The INDEPENDENT person will be irked and irritated if the REALIST tries to involve him/her too much in material detail and practical chores and decisions.

The key to success in this relationship is to enjoy your separate identities without losing emotional contact with each other.

44

Pleasure-seeking and Dynamic

The attraction is powerful in this combination. The DYNAMIC person needs praise, attention and proof of his/her desirability; and the PLEASURE-SEEKER enjoys giving warmth and love and making his/her partner happy.

Interests may clash sometimes. For the PLEASURE-SEEKER may not always take the DYNAMIC person's driving spirit and ambition seriously enough, often finding it boring to live with someone who is so absorbed in work and self-improvement, and being unable to sympathize with DYNAMIC's nervous tension, strong feelings and inability to relax enough.

The DYNAMIC person may very often be too consumed with his/her pursuits to provide the diversion and entertainment the PLEASURE-SEEKER needs. However, unless this is taken to extremes, the PLEASURE-SEEKING person will be able to cope. He/she is usually tolerant and easy-going and can therefore forgive the short temper, scenes and hostilities of the DYNAMIC person.

The DYNAMIC person in his/her more relaxed moods can enjoy the company of the PLEASURE-SEEKER. There is a lot of scope for fun and adventure in this relationship. The PLEASURE-SEEKER gets on well with people and makes a good impression on them, and this is a very important quality which the DYNAMIC partner appreciates. Sexually and socially this is probably an excellent combination, though it is unlikely to be a deeply emotional union.

Tender-hearted and Independent

This is a difficult combination because your needs are so different, and it's doubtful whether either of you could compromise enough to make the relationship work in the long term.

The TENDER-HEARTED person looks for love and

security, for emotional closeness, for shared interests and experiences, and for a life-style which incorporates as much togetherness as possible. The INDEPENDENT person seeks freedom and self-expression, and such a self-sufficient person would find it difficult to understand the emotional needs of a TENDER-HEARTED partner. He/she might begin to find the relationship cloying and restricting.

The TENDER-HEARTED partner is likely to find the relationship cold and emotionally unrewarding. As the INDEPENDENT person doesn't need people very much, and the TENDER-HEARTED person is likely to be rather reserved, you may sometimes find social life a problem.

This combination of an emotional person and a rational person may be fascinating to both at first, but a lot of understanding and compromising is necessary in order to evolve a way of life to suit you both.

Realistic and Pleasure-seeking
In many ways this could be a good relationship. The PLEASURE-SEEKER brings fun and enjoyment into the REALIST's life, and as you are both likely to be sexually uninhibited the physical side of the relationship should be very satisfying to both of you.

The REALIST can take over the planning and decisions. He/she will enjoy taking responsibility for the relationship and will feel needed and appreciated. The PLEASURE-SEEKER is only too happy to hand over responsibility to the REALIST, especially in married life.

You are both cheerful and optimistic, responsive to the outside world and interested in people and events around you, so you should gain pleasure and stimulation in each other's company and enjoy the same kind of outings, activities, and so on.

However, there *are* possible conflicts. If the REALIST has a strict or conventional moral code he/she may sometimes disapprove of the PLEASURE-SEEKER's lack of self-discipline, and begin to see him/her as immature, lazy, greedy, morally-weak, etc. The REALIST may then attempt to be a parent figure of authority, curbing the wayward qualities of the PLEASURE-SEEKER and becoming both over-critical and over-protective. The PLEASURE-SEEKER will react badly to this, losing patience with the REALIST's spartan, kill-joy attitudes, and resenting the heavy-handed treatment and restriction of freedom.

It would certainly be easier if the REALIST were the one who did the adapting and compromising. The PLEASURE-SEEKER would be full of very good intentions, but it is not in his/her nature to be consistent in making the effort required to tone down and become more 'sensible'.

Dynamic and Romantic

A beautiful relationship in many ways, and probably quite ecstatic in its early stages. The instant attraction stems from the fact that you both want to be special, remarkable people, and you both have the gift of making each other feel wonderful. In the DYNAMIC person the ROMANTIC can see someone to look up to and admire. The DYNAMIC partner enjoys the admiration and will be quite bowled over by the ROMANTIC's emotional excesses and seductive style of loving. The combination of DYNAMIC passion and ROMANTIC spiritual love will be very exciting and add new dimensions to your lives.

If this relationship sounds too good to be true, there *are* pitfalls and difficulties which may emerge after the first flush of romance. As you both tend to be egotistical and demanding at times, jealousy may crop up. Each partner may want to prove that he/she is more attractive than the other, and emotional traumas are bound to be the result.

The DYNAMIC person is far more active and realistic than the ROMANTIC and may become irritated with the ROMANTIC's inconsistent emotions and seeming lack of drive and purpose. The ROMANTIC will feel neglected when DYNAMIC is too busy and preoccupied with his/her 'selfish' interests to pay enough attention to the relationship.

On the whole an exciting love-hate relationship with wonderful good patches and rather dreadful and dramatic bad patches.

Realistic and Tender-hearted

This is an attraction of opposites, which is powerful and emotionally satisfying to both of you in different ways; your differences complementing each other and drawing you close together rather than causing you to grow apart.

You have a lot to give each other and you both genuinely and naturally want to gratify each other's needs and desires.

From the TENDER-HEARTED person's point of view, his/her partner is caring and considerate and kind, easy to admire and respect, to rely on and to trust. So TENDER-HEARTED finds everything he/she is looking for—the emotional comfort and stability, the sense of belonging, loyalty and closeness. In these circumstances TENDER-HEARTED can release and express all his/her deep love and affection, even adoration.

The REALISTIC person is delighted and flattered. It gives him/her great satisfaction to know that TENDER-HEARTED admires and trusts his/her strong opinions and judgements. TENDER-HEARTED's emotional warmth and powerful but quiet passion also bring a new and rewarding experience into the life and feelings of the REALIST, who gains understanding and emotional insight from the relationship.

This is a combination of clearly-defined roles, where the REALISTIC person is recognized as the dominant partner, and the TENDER-HEARTED person is recognized as the more gentle and submissive, giving love and tenderness in return for guidance and protection.

Both of you should gain a lot of emotional fulfilment as long as the roles don't become *too* routine-bound and inflexible.

Romantic and Pleasure-seeking
You both live for love, idealize it and weave your fantasies around it, so the combination of romantic love and sensual love should be a highly exciting and rewarding experience for you both. Sex is likely to dominate the relationship almost exclusively at the beginning, but you will find other sources of pleasure and satisfaction in the relationship, too.

The ROMANTIC person, craving for glamour but not always being extraverted enough to do anything about it, will benefit from the PLEASURE-SEEKER's ease in making social contacts, and his/her ability in always seeming to know where all the fun, action and excitement are. The PLEASURE-SEEKER gains understanding and novelty-value from the ROMANTIC outlook on life.

You both share the same dislike for detail and routine, you are both easily bored and anxious for varied experience in life, so you will spur each other on in the pursuit of social adventures and good times.

The ROMANTIC partner is more emotional than the PLEASURE-SEEKER, and any conflicts are most likely to be a result of the ROMANTIC partner feeling jealous and over-sensitive, taking the PLEASURE-SEEKER'S faults too personally and too seriously.

The main danger is that the pace of the relationship is so fast that it may burn itself out. Generally, it seems a more sensible relationship for a love affair or holiday romance, rather than for marriage. As a long-term combination neither of you would be much help to the other in adjusting to the hard and drab realities of everyday life when routine and responsibility enter into your lives.

Independent and Dynamic

You are both self-willed in your different ways and can admire aspects of each other's personalities. You can interest each other and influence each other constructively.

The INDEPENDENT can help to give stability and a more rational view of life, ideas and theories which the DYNAMIC person can put into action. So the INDEPENDENT partner brings reason and mental stimulation into the relationship. The DYNAMIC person has an enlivening effect on the INDEPENDENT and helps him/her to be more sociable and demonstrative.

There are possible sources of conflict and irritation on both sides of the relationship. The INDEPENDENT person may sometimes be irritated by the DYNAMIC's emphasis on material success and status, by his/her anxiety to impress others and occasional lack of integrity.

The DYNAMIC partner may complain about lack of communication and boredom in the relationship when his/her partner withdraws into a private world and doesn't seem to need company. Being rather an egotist, DYNAMIC may sometimes feel starved of praise and appreciation.

Basically, though, there is a lot of freedom within the relationship, and it should work well if both partners are willing to compromise up to a point—the DYNAMIC person by trying not to demand too much or impose his/her will too much, and the INDEPENDENT person by trying to accept a certain amount of demanding behaviour, and giving in to loss of privacy sometimes. Neither of you needs an excessive amount of emotional support, so this is not an intensely close relationship. But you are both free to expand your personalities and individual aims. In the long term this means that you are likely to find each other interesting as people, and you can perhaps avoid the staleness of over-familiarity.

Romantic and Realistic

This is an attraction of opposites. The REALIST will be charmed·and intrigued by the imagination and unpredictable emotions of the ROMANTIC. The ROMANTIC will be attracted by the REALIST's strength of character and air of authority.

The REALIST will find amusement and entertainment, and the ROMANTIC will find emotional honesty and a sense of security.

You have a lot to give each other, and in an ideal situation you should allow each other to express your emotional needs. The ROMANTIC's ego will be satisfied because he/she is allowed to be the exotic, colourful and showy personality of the couple, and the one who brings a sense of beauty and romantic love into the relationship. The REALIST will benefit from this and also from the fact that he/she is allowed to be the strong controlling influence, the one who is respected and looked up to as the capable organizer.

The main danger is that you may begin to lose sympathy with each other because your outlooks on life are so different. The REALIST may lose respect for someone as illogical and inconsistent as the ROMANTIC, seeing him/her as emotionally shallow and immature. The ROMANTIC may find many fond illusions about life shattered by the REALIST's hard attitudes and moralistic judgements.

Effort may be needed to understand each other and to meet half way. As long as you continue to appreciate each other's different styles and as long as you can both make compromises sometimes, this could be a good relationship.

Dynamic and Tender-hearted

An attraction of opposites which could lead to an emotionally successful relationship. The TENDER-HEARTED is someone who usually identifies very closely with his/her partner. So he/she will be delighted at the success of the DYNAMIC person, and sympathetic in the event of failure.

The TENDER-HEARTED person will be proud of the DYNAMIC and take a genuine interest in all aspects of the DYNAMIC's life and personality. The DYNAMIC person will be both flattered and comforted by the loving attention of the TENDER-HEARTED.

The DYNAMIC person can be passionate, but is not consistently emotional. However, in this combination it is often possible for him/her to express emotion and to become more aware of deep feelings. In this way the TENDER-HEARTED can add a new dimension to the DYNAMIC partner's emotional life, and the DYNAMIC partner can provide stimulation and an exciting life-style.

It would be wise for the TENDER-HEARTED person to realize there will be times when the DYNAMIC partner might be difficult to live with, impatient and neglectful, not always needing closeness and emotional support. The DYNAMIC person should realize that his/her partner responds to love and kindness and needs to be deeply involved.

It is important that the TENDER-HEARTED partner develops interests and activities outside the relationship so that he/she is not too dependent on the DYNAMIC partner. This will prevent the DYNAMIC partner from feeling too restless and trapped.

Pleasure-seeking and Independent

This is a combination of two very different people, with very different outlooks and aims in life. It is an attraction of opposites.

In the short term at least the relationship has a great novelty-value for both of you, and you would enjoy introducing each other to your different life-styles, giving each other new experiences.

The INDEPENDENT person can gain fun and sensual enjoyment from the relationship, and perhaps through sexual pleasure be enabled to forget his/her troubles and more serious preoccupations in life. So the relationship is something of a holiday for the INDEPENDENT, allowing him/her to relax, to shake off inhibition and express the sensual side of his/her personality. The PLEASURE-SEEKER may well feel a 'wicked' sense of joy in leading the INDEPENDENT person astray; the novelty is exciting and even if the PLEASURE-SEEKER finds it difficult to understand the INDEPENDENT's behaviour and feelings sometimes, there will be a sense of curiosity and challenge, and also a feeling of respect.

As a long-term relationship though this is an unusual and difficult combination, and the dangers are many. To the PLEASURE-SEEKER the INDEPENDENT person may begin to appear 'shut-in', lacking vitality, his/her view of life too serious and intellectual, and his/her sense of fun and humour lacking.

To the INDEPENDENT person the PLEASURE-SEEKER may begin to seem superficial, lacking depth and interest, their view of life limited and too self-indulgent.

Interests may clash so much that you may lose contact with each other, so great tolerance and understanding are necessary on both sides to make the relationship work.

Realistic and Dynamic
This is a combination of two strong personalities, both with very definite ideas about what sort of people you are and what kind of lives you want to lead.

If you can both be tolerant and agree about the important things in your lives this could be a very successful long-term relationship. You are equals. You respect each other and provide interest and challenge for each other. You are both self-confident and you can both be quite tough at times, so you can have angry scenes and be evenly matched; neither of you will be too hurt or deflated.

The dangers are that the REALISTIC partner may find the DYNAMIC unreasonable and hot-headed at times; also selfish and childishly demanding in wanting his/her own way. The DYNAMIC partner may sometimes be irritated and impatient with the REALIST's sensible and responsible attitudes, seeing him/her as stuffy and self-righteous.

The DYNAMIC partner may be grateful for the REALIST's help and moral support when things are difficult, but resent the same help and support when it is not wanted or needed. The REALIST is likely to find this hard to take. However, if you can come to terms with each other and make allowances for each other's personalities, this could be a lively and enjoyable relationship with room for freedom to follow your separate interests and also to share aims and interests.

Tender-hearted and Pleasure-seeking
The initial attraction is likely to be very strong and satisfying in this combination. The natural kindness, warmth and spontaneous love of the PLEASURE-SEEKER will be very attractive to the TENDER-HEARTED. Sharing the PLEASURE-SEEKER's sense of fun, sensual pleasure and sociable life-style will also be a very enjoyable experience.

From the PLEASURE-SEEKER's point of view he/she gains satisfaction from the loyalty, sentimentality and emotional love of the TENDER-HEARTED. So the combination of sensual and emotional expressiveness can make for a very happy relationship. The problem will be whether you can maintain this level of mutual appreciation and satisfaction.

The PLEASURE-SEEKER needs variety and excitement and may begin to feel trapped and restricted by his/her partner's desire for loyalty and closeness. The PLEASURE-SEEKER may begin to find the responsibility of the relationship rather a burden.

The TENDER-HEARTED may begin to fear the PLEASURE-SEEKER's unfaithfulness and will be tempted to react by becoming clinging and suspicious, longing for emotional fulfilment and communication.

However, if you can both guard against these dangers and strike a balance between the pursuit of pleasure and the need for emotional trust and togetherness, this will be a good relationship.

Independent and Romantic
In some ways this is an attraction of opposites, and yet you are both basically caring and sensitive enough to recognize each other's needs.

The INDEPENDENT partner will be charmed by the ROMANTIC's emotional expressiveness, spontaneity and imagination. The ROMANTIC, who looks for someone to be proud of, will be impressed by the INDEPENDENT person's quiet strength of character and his/her possible intellectual superiority.

Your outlooks on life are very different, one being logical and the other being fanciful and intuitive, so although you can stimulate and interest each other mentally and emotionally, you will sometimes find it hard to understand each other. The ROMANTIC tends to exaggerate his/her feelings, while the INDEPENDENT tends to understate them, and this may lead to misunderstandings.

The INDEPENDENT partner may begin to find the ROMANTIC vain and emotionally demanding, while the ROMANTIC may find the INDEPENDENT remote and over-critical.

The INDEPENDENT person should remember that the ROMANTIC craves for love, applause and attention, and the ROMANTIC person should remember that the INDEPENDENT needs privacy and freedom.

You both have a lot of insight in different ways and this should help you to keep in touch with each other emotionally, and to be aware of each other's feelings and desires. It won't always be an easy combination, but it has deeply rewarding possibilities.

FIRST IMPRESSIONS QUIZ

How do you judge people? What do you notice about them? Every time you look at someone you form an impression of them, however vague and fleeting. Sometimes perhaps you make quite a hobby out of people-watching, becoming fascinated by faces in a crowd and playing the psychological detective to deduce what sort of people they are, what sort of lives they lead.

However, the judgements you make about most strangers around you most of the time are usually so instinctive that you are hardly aware of any analyzing process at all. In fact your snap judgements probably tell far more about *you* than about the people you're watching.

Imagine you are taking a long bus ride, and the following fourteen people sit opposite you at various stages during your journey. You couldn't help looking at them and forming some kind of opinion or emotional reaction.

Look at each portrait and read the set of comments below. Tick the one you feel would be nearest to your reaction to the person depicted.

I.

(d) Independent and defensive. Had a deprived childhood, and has struggled out of it, but still has a chip on
his shoulder.

(b) Looks shifty and dishonest, maybe even has criminal
tendencies.

(a) He's shrewd and self-made, probably runs a small
business, drives a hard bargain.

(c) He looks tough and aggressive, but there's something
sad about him. He's more sensitive than he looks.

2.

(b) Nice, friendly-looking girl!

(c) She looks very happy. I think she's in love.

(d) Comes from a nice, conventional family—simple view of life, limited mental horizons.

(a) Probably a secretary in her first job, very neat and conscientious, but will choose marriage rather than a career.

(c) A very kind person who would always go out of his way to help you. He is sensitive and can be moody too, though.

(a) Ineffectual! He'll never get very far—he's dominated by his mother or his wife.

(d) Conservative in outlook, strong sense of duty, sits on committees and worries about pollution.

(b) Rather reserved, but pleasant and likable.

(a) Plenty of guts and spirit—will fight to get what she wants.
(d) Rather a shallow, materialistic nature.
(b) Good looking and knows it—has an active sex life.
(c) Fun-loving and self-confident, but could be rather hard and selfish.

5.

(b) A typical ex-public school bore!

(a) Enviable really—young, attractive, rich and privileged too!

(c) Too smooth and conceited—he really thinks he's wonderful.

(d) He feels very grand going out to work with his briefcase and umbrella, but he's not so sure of himself, emotionally immature.

6.

(c) A very sympathetic, loyal girl, understands people, would be a good friend and you could confide in her.

(a) Refined, has good taste, intelligent, probably went to a private school.

(d) Aesthetic and artistic, discriminating, rather shy emotionally.

(b) Looks a bit glum and gloomy to me!

(a) Ordinary sort of man, works hard, talks a lot, spends a lot of time in the pub.

(d) Free from pressure or worry—has accepted himself and his life but is rather dogmatic.

(b) Very nice face, cheerful and honest.

(c) Loves his wife and children, has a very happy family life.

8.

(d) What's she doing on a bus? Perhaps the Rolls has broken down, or the chauffeur's got measles!

(a) That coat must've cost a small fortune! I wonder who she is . . .

(c) Very intimidating, aloof and unsympathetic.

(b) You can't help resenting that type—totally out of touch with the real world.

(c) He doesn't look at all happy. He's worried or his girl friend has let him down or something.

(d) All the problems of extended adolescence, but there's a lot of potential; has spiritual values.

(b) The intellectual type!

(a) His parents are ambitious for him. He's probably training to be a solicitor or accountant.

(b) Bitter and slovenly.

(d) A victim of circumstance, without the strength of character to cope.

(a) Not the sort of person I could relate to in any way— she wouldn't occupy my thoughts at all if I saw her on a bus really.

(c) She looks so ill and tired and miserable. I feel sorry for her, but can't help being a little bit repulsed, too.

(d) An interesting person, intelligent, freedom-loving and broad-minded.

(c) Lively personality, he gets on well with people and has a lot of friends.

(a) A theatrical type who is probably a bit of a has-been. All talk and not much action.

(b) Rather a crank, trying to be too young and trendy for his age.

(c) She looks calm and serene with a lot of inner strength. She is contented with her life.

(a) A rather dull housewife type, I should think.

(b) A do-gooding type, religious and highly principled.

(d) Efficient and methodical, has a practical, undemanding outlook on life.

(b) The sporting type—all outdoors and adventure.
(c) Very warm-hearted and charming—falls in love easily.
(d) Very forceful appearance, not a great thinker but he's active and enterprising.
(a) Dynamic and ambitious, working his way up in his firm and keen to prove himself.

(d) Perceptive; instinctive rather than academic in-
    telligence.
(b) Rather bossy-looking, too proud and demanding.
(a) Very sharp, a self-starter, knows what she wants.
(c) A very emotional, passionate nature, spontaneous and
    impulsive.

Now count your score, mainly (a) (b) (c) or (d) and turn
to the CONCLUSIONS.

CONCLUSIONS

Mostly (a)

Your first impressions of people are governed by a desire to know where they stand in the social hierarchy in terms of cla..s, material success and achievement. You look for the outward signs of status through people's appearance, clothes and general demeanour. When you evaluate people you are interested in their jobs, their financial position, their possessions, their life-style and the other people who form their social group.

Through habit and experience in summing people up in this way, you can probably get a very rapid mental picture of their position and status relative to yours. Whether your conclusions are right or not, it is important to you to form an opinion, which will then determine the way you deal with and approach others.

Once you have placed them in the social structure you can then begin to think about their characteristics and personal qualities.

Being an admirer of achievement, the qualities associated with success are those which you notice first and respond to most.

You will notice someone's air of self-confidence, self-assertion or sophistication, for instance. In reverse your attention will be drawn to someone's seeming lack of drive and initiative, to their air of diffidence or submissiveness, to the signs of lower status than your own. This doesn't mean you'll dislike them for it, but it *will* affect the initial course of your relationship with them, and it *will* tend to over-shadow their other qualities. It is quite likely that you sometimes miss out on potentially good relationships because of this. Once you have 'down-graded' someone it will be more difficult to appreciate their good qualities and more difficult to recognize the mutual sympathies and things you have in common with them.

Perhaps you also tend to exaggerate the good qualities

of people you have hall-marked as successful, and to imagine that their lives are far happier and more perfect than they really are.

You naturally expect others to judge you in the same way that you judge them, so that your image in the eyes of others is a very important preoccupation in your life. You are very conscious of being judged. You constantly measure yourself against others, anxious to gauge your comparative popularity, attractiveness, ability, success and so on.

If you yourself feel successful, or at least hopeful that one day your aspirations will be realized, you will be more generous and tolerant in your judgements of people, but you may experience some bitterness or envy when you feel socially disadvantaged. Otherwise you are generally competitive in a friendly kind of way, willing to give others credit for their attributes and achievements.

Of course people's circumstances do affect their personalities, but there is a danger of placing too much emphasis on their circumstances and too little emphasis on their more abiding and deeper qualities. However, on closer acquaintance with people you will certainly begin to attach more importance to their intrinsic personalities and less to their position in society.

Mostly (b)
Your first impressions of people are instant and spontaneous and your reactions to them are honest and direct. Someone's physical appearance makes an immediate impact on you, and you make instinctive judgements about their general character from the way they look.

. Although your reactions to people are emotional, they are not very deeply felt in a personal sense. You tend not to compare yourself with others in terms of social status or personal qualities. Unless there is a possibility of having at least a casual relationship with people you are not normally curious about their backgrounds or about the details of their lives, where they live, what their job is, what kind of friends they have and so on.

Your instinctive concern is whether you like or dislike someone, whether you judge them as good people or bad people, whether they are attractive or unattractive to you, whether their faces give you a fleeting feeling of pleasure or displeasure, and whether they evoke a sense of approval or disapproval.

So your likes and dislikes can be very strong, and your moral judgements can be rather harsh and unqualified.

You tend to put people into stereotypes, probably based on your previous experiences of relationships and the way you have categorized people in the past.

Because someone has a beard, for instance, they must be friendly/hiding something/boastful and brash/or whatever your preconceptions of men with beards happen to be. Of course everyone builds up these automatic preconceptions to a degree, but there is always a danger of getting stuck in an attitude about someone and being unable to overcome it; of judging *too much* too dogmatically on too little evidence.

Because of this you may be inclined to dismiss people without giving them a chance. Your initial impression of them is likely to prejudice your views about them even on closer acquaintance. You form strong opinions very quickly and it is likely that once you have formed an opinion you find it hard to switch your feelings and change your attitudes.

Your feelings are decisive and rather uncompromising; you don't often make allowances for people; tending not to take extenuating circumstances into account when judging people's behaviour and actions.

You are probably tough in your response to other people's judgement of you. You would certainly be very loath to admit much concern about the impression you make on others. When you are criticized you are likely to see it as a reflection of the other person's state of mind, rather than any real reflection of your own personality.

73

Having such definite emotional responses to people, you are likely to be a very good friend and a rather formidable enemy!

Mostly (c)
Your first impressions of people are highly personal and emotional in content. You see people in terms of how they would relate to you, what they would think of you, the kind of relationship you would have with them if you were to get to know them.

You attach little importance to the material aspect of people's lives, or to their status and position in society. Although you may bring your imagination to bear on the circumstances of their lives you are primarily interested in their qualities of personality, what sort of people they are rather than what they do and what they own.

You are interested in their emotional state, and you look for points of sympathy and contact with them, comparing their probable feelings to your own, and noticing their similarities and their differences, using emotional rather than moral standards in order to gauge how much you would like someone and how much you would have in common with them.

It is likely that you make quite a hobby out of people-watching, and can become absorbed in speculation about them. You are genuinely fascinated by people, responding to them in a deeply emotional way. Even in the most casual encounter—asking someone the time, buying something from someone in a shop, being approached by a market-research person, being very briefly introduced to someone—you respond to them on a very personal level, feeling perhaps excessively warm after a friendly encounter and excessively put-out, angry or deflated after a hostile one. Being extremely sensitive to people and aware of their emotional tone, you are likely to gain very real insights on a hit-and-miss basis, though you are not objective enough to be a consistently good judge of character. You are likely either to idealize people or else to be too swayed by your unfavourable impressions of them.

In all you are thoughtful and intuitive in your reactions to people, failing to be analytical, but more than making up for that by creative speculation and imagination which sometimes become rather far removed from reality.

You are curious about people's feelings, about their social lives, their love lives. The qualities you notice first and to which you respond most are those to do with relationships. You are concerned about how sincere someone is likely to be, how friendly, gregarious, sympathetic, emotionally responsive they are, and most important perhaps, you want to know how they would react to you and whether they are on the same wavelength as you.

In real relationships you are adaptable to others and flexible in your attitudes. Your opinion of someone may change quite radically as the relationship progresses; people you dislike at first may grow on you; you will then be willing to admit you misjudged them. People you liked at first may prove disappointing to you; you will then blame yourself for failing to see through them. So although you are loyal and steadfast once a friendship has become fairly solid, you can expect emotional changes before that stage has been reached.

You expect others to judge you as emotionally as you judge them, and of course you are very sensitive to other people's opinions of you. You possibly tend to over-estimate the strength of their reactions to you, forgetting that not everyone is as emotional as you are. You will be inclined to imagine great admiration or scorn, intense liking or disliking, where in fact people's view of you in general will be far more casual and far less dramatic than you think.

Mostly (d)
Your first impressions of people are based on an objective appraisal of them. You are observant and analytical, able

to dissect people in a cool but often imaginative way; your emotional reaction to a stranger very often being less important than your 'detective work' and logical summing-up.

You are curious about people's backgrounds and life-styles, about the kind of work they do and the kind of relationships they have. You are interested in their past and present circumstances, and concerned about placing them with reasonable accuracy in the social structure.

This is not because you are specially interested in measuring their social status against yours, but because you feel you need this information in order to discover their way of thinking; their general attitudes and philosophy of life. The things about people which you notice and admire are the signs of independent thinking, individuality, intellect and originality. The things you notice and dislike are qualities like dullness, rigid values and conventionality.

You tend not to make moral judgements, so you are not concerned in general whether people are 'nice' or 'nasty', but you enjoy speculating on whether people are witty, good company, lucid and fluent talkers, inventive, creative, imaginative and so on.

You are inclined to be fairly impersonal in your judgements, especially in cases where you decide that the other person's mental processes and attitudes are very different from your own. You are far more concerned about what *you* think of *them* than about what they are likely to think of you.

Until you form a relationship with someone, you tend to view people's emotions in somewhat coldly psychological terms. Deep involvements with people take time, and there is a danger of standing on the outside viewing others rather like interesting exhibits. This tendency to shut out your feelings may sometimes give the impression of snobbishness and aloofness, yet with people whom you judge to be on your own level you can gain an instant rapport.

You will certainly be discriminating in your choice of friends, and very loyal to those you have picked out to be close to you.

Being a rather self-directed person who may dismiss conventional standards it is unlikely that you worry very much what the world in general thinks of you. However, when you respect someone and value his/her judgement you will be as concerned as anyone else about the impression you are making.

TROUBLE AND BOTHER QUIZ

Relationships can run into all kinds of difficulty where resentment builds up and misunderstandings abound. When this happens the natural reaction is to blame the state of the relationship on to the other person or people involved, because it's much easier (and also much less painful) to see other people's faults than to see your own.

But you may well find that the same sorts of conflict and tension tend to crop up in your relationships with all kinds of different person. So various aspects of your own personality make you susceptible to specific kinds of problem in your relationships. These may apply equally to casual relationships through friendships to your close emotional relationships, your lover/marriage partner, your children and members of your own family.

Honesty is an important virtue in answering this Quiz to find out what the problem areas in your relationships are likely to be. So be as truthful and realistic as possible in your replies!

1. Does it irritate you when your partner/a friend mispronounces a word or uses it in the wrong context?
    Strong Yes ☐   Only Mildly ☐   Strong No ☐
2. Do you ever feel pangs of envy when you see couples of your own age kissing or displaying affection for each other in public?
    Strong Yes ☐   Only Mildly ☐   Strong No ☐
3. Do you feel it is slovenly and rather shameful to lie in bed for too long in the mornings?
    Strong Yes ☐   Only Mildly ☐   Strong No ☐
4. Do you ever feel that people react more favourably towards you when you are with your partner than when you are on your own?
    Strong Yes ☐   Sometimes ☐   Strong No ☐
5. Do you often feel you 'can't be bothered' to chat to people?
    Strong Yes ☐   Sometimes ☐   Strong No ☐

6. Do you feel self-conscious about combing your hair/ blowing your nose/tying up your shoe-lace, etc. in public?
   Strong Yes ☐ Only Mildly ☐ Strong No ☐

7. Are you ever conscious that you are 'fishing' for compliments or boasting unduly?
   Strong Yes ☐ Sometimes ☐ Strong No ☐

8. Do you dislike having to change your usual brand of coffee/tea/beer/wine/or any other commercial product?
   Strong Yes ☐ Only Mildly ☐ Strong No ☐

9. Do you often find it hard to make small decisions?
   Strong Yes ☐ Sometimes ☐ Strong No ☐

10. Do you feel generally that people who make a big display of their emotions are shallow or insincere?
    Strong Yes ☐ Sometimes ☐ Strong No ☐

11. Do you feel ashamed of your partner if he/she is dressed in bad taste, or unsuitably for the occasion?
    Strong Yes ☐ Only Mildly ☐ Strong No ☐

12. Do you enjoy and frequently indulge in 'gossiping' sessions about other people?
    Strong Yes ☐ Sometimes ☐ Strong No ☐

13. Do you have high standards of tidiness and hygiene?
    Strong Yes ☐ Only Mildly ☐ Strong No ☐

14. Do you feel you have changed quite a bit (in your emotional reactions or your general attitudes) since you have been with your present partner?
    Strong Yes ☐ Only Mildly ☐ Strong No ☐

15. Do you often feel lonely and 'out of things' in a crowd of people/friends?
    Strong Yes ☐ Sometimes ☐ Strong No ☐

16. Do you find it very embarrassing when couples quarrel in front of you?
    Strong Yes ☐ Only Mildly ☐ Strong No ☐

17. In a group of friends, are you ever conscious of talking simply because you want to dominate the con-

versation, rather than because you have something you want to say?

Strong Yes ☐   Sometimes   ☐   Strong No ☐

18. Do you get irritated when someone leaves caps off toothpaste tubes/leaves the newspaper on the sofa, etc?

Strong Yes ☐   Only Mildly ☐   Strong No ☐

19. Do you constantly change your mind about what you think of your friends and how much you like them?

Strong Yes ☐   Sometimes   ☐   Strong No ☐

20. Do you feel the need for time and privacy to 'get into yourself' and think your thoughts?

Strong Yes ☐   Sometimes   ☐   Strong No ☐

21. Would you feel disadvantaged if you 'bumped into' a very smart, well-dressed friend when you were looking untidily and cheaply-dressed?

Strong Yes ☐   Only Mildly ☐   Strong No ☐

22. Do you enjoy talking about yourself, telling strangers your life story, and so on?

Strong Yes ☐   Sometimes   ☐   Strong No ☐

23. Do you hate eating earlier or later than your normal times?

Strong Yes ☐   Only Mildly ☐   Strong No ☐

24. Do you find it difficult to join in discussions/arguments because you're not quite sure what your opinions really are on many subjects?

Strong Yes ☐   Sometimes   ☐   Strong No ☐

25. Do you pick and choose carefully the people to whom you confide and divulge personal information?

Strong Yes ☐   Sometimes   ☐   Strong No ☐

26. Do you feel embarrassed when a companion engages you in a personal conversation in a loud voice in public?

Strong Yes ☐   Only Mildly ☐   Strong No ☐

27. Do you feel upset and jealous when a more attractive member of your own sex steals the limelight in a group of mixed company?

Strong Yes ☐   Only Mildly ☐   Strong No ☐

28. Do you dislike lending and borrowing?
Strong Yes ☐   Only Mildly ☐   Strong No ☐

29. Do you tend to take both advice and criticism very seriously and to heart?
Strong Yes ☐   Only Mildly ☐   Strong No ☐

30. In a group conversation do you often find you have gone into a train of thought of your own, unrelated to the topic being discussed?
Strong Yes ☐   Sometimes ☐   Strong No ☐

31. When your marriage/relationship is going through a bad patch, do you tend to talk to your friends as though everything is all right?
Strong Yes ☐   Sometimes ☐   Strong No ☐

32. Do you get into a state of panic/distress at the thought of going grey/bald/fat/wrinkled/losing your looks?
Strong Yes ☐   Only Mildly ☐   Strong No ☐

33. If you fail to carry out all the chores you'd planned for the day, do you feel very displeased with yourself?
Strong Yes ☐   Only Mildly ☐   Strong No ☐

34. Do you often get drawn into situations or friendships which you are not really happy about?
Strong Yes ☐   Sometimes ☐   Strong No ☐

35. Do you often avoid expressing your feelings because you feel people wouldn't understand?
Strong Yes ☐   Sometimes ☐   Strong No ☐

36. Do you often compare your partner's social status and/or financial standing with that of your friend's partners?
Strong Yes ☐   Sometimes ☐   Strong No ☐

37. Do you feel the need to be romantically in love either overtly or secretly in your mind all the time?
Strong Yes ☐   Sometimes ☐   Strong No ☐

38. Do you feel guilty if you forget to keep even a small, unimportant promise?
Strong Yes ☐   Only Mildly ☐   Strong No ☐

39. When someone has treated you badly do you usually find you can forgive them quite easily?
Strong Yes ☐   Sometimes ☐   Strong No ☐

40. Do you often find it difficult to give people your full attention when they are telling you something or explaining something to you?
Strong Yes ☐   Sometimes ☐   Strong No ☐

41. Do you feel wretched when you make a social *faux pas*, i.e. using the wrong fork/spilling your wine/making a silly remark/not understanding the formalities at a wedding/grand dinner/office function etc.?
Strong Yes ☐   Only Mildly ☐   Strong No ☐

42. Are you inclined to exaggerate and embroider true stories and anecdotes in the telling?
Strong Yes ☐   Only Mildly   Strong No ☐

43. Do you often find it hard to understand how people get into such a muddle with their lives?
Strong Yes ☐   Sometimes ☐   Strong No ☐

44. Do you often wish you possessed qualities you admire in certain friends/acquaintances?
Strong Yes ☐   Sometimes ☐   Strong No ☐

45. Do you tend to feel uncomfortable when strangers force intimacy and tell you their life story?
Strong Yes ☐   Only Mildly ☐   Strong No ☐

Now see SCORING PAGE.

SCORING PAGE

This quiz should now be divided into five sections according to the question numbers set out below.

In each case   Strong Yes   = 3 Points
              Only Mildly/
              or Sometimes = 2 Points
              Strong No   = 1 Point

Fill in the number of points you have scored for each question in the boxes below, add the total for each section and then turn to the conclusions.

SECTION ONE		SECTION TWO	
Question Number	Number of Points	Question Number	Number of Points
1 = ☐		2 = ☐	
6 = ☐		7 = ☐	
11 = ☐		12 = ☐	
16 = ☐		17 = ☐	
21 = ☐		22 = ☐	
26 = ☐		27 = ☐	
31 = ☐		32 = ☐	
36 = ☐		37 = ☐	
41 = ☐		42 = ☐	
Total =		Total =	

SECTION THREE			SECTION FOUR	
Question Number	Number of Points		Question Number	Number of Points
3 = ☐			4 = ☐	
8 = ☐			9 = ☐	
13 = ☐			14 = ☐	
18 = ☐			19 = ☐	
23 = ☐			24 = ☐	
28 = ☐			29 = ☐	
33 = ☐			34 = ☐	
38 = ☐			39 = ☐	
43 = ☐			44 = ☐	
Total = ———			Total = ———	

SECTION FIVE	
Question Number	Number of Points
5 = ☐	
10 = ☐	
15 = ☐	
20 = ☐	
25 = ☐	
30 = ☐	
35 = ☐	
40 = ☐	
45 = ☐	
Total = ———	

SECTION ONE—CONVENTION

When there is trouble in a relationship it is convenient to blame the other person for not coming up to your expectations, but the question to ask yourself is whether you are forgetting the real human issues and judging the other person purely by conventional standards.

For instance, the mother says to her child, 'Why can't you be like So-and-So? So-and-So behaves himself and works hard, so why don't you?'

The child's naughtiness is seen simply as a failure to measure up to someone else, rather than as a result of his/her own personality and emotional reactions.

Of course conventional standards are useful in giving you a guideline in conducting your relationships, but external standards shouldn't be taken too seriously at the expense of your appreciation of the other person's individuality.

If you scored 22–27 points in this section tensions and resentments may arise in your relationships partly because you tend to judge the other person's actions and behaviour by conventional standards rather than individual ones. So if the other person doesn't conform to your preconceptions you are inclined to be too ready to blame and criticize, without looking any further into your own feelings, or into the needs and feelings of your partner.

It will therefore be difficult for you to understand the other person's motives, because you will pre-judge rather than trying to analyze the situation. It will also be difficult for you to make allowances for the other person, who may or may not have very real problems and grievances of their own. The trouble is that if you hide too much behind conventional standards it becomes very hard to come to grips with the relationship on a more personal and emotional level.

You tend to look at the relationship from the *outside*, in other words to view it as you think other people view it. You are inclined to be too self-conscious about the relationship; too concerned about what the world thinks of you as a couple; too preoccupied with what you think the relationship *ought* to be, rather than what it actually *is*.

Up to a point of course everyone is concerned about their image as a couple, and it's impossible really to see yourselves unrelated to the rest of the world. Everyone sees their relationships in context to the social scene around them, and in relation to their friends, neighbours and acquaintances. But at the same time it's good to realize that the important aspects of relationships are private and not particularly for public display—your inward feelings, for instance, of happiness or despair, of unity or discord, which the rest of the world doesn't see and doesn't know about.

Another difficulty which stems from the desire to 'keep up appearances' is that as long as relationships are running smoothly on the surface, you may not delve any deeper.

When there are emotional problems you may be tempted to gloss over them instead of acknowledging and trying to do something about them.

In general it would be worth trying to understand your own and other people's motives as stemming more from individual personality, and less from the rules and expectations of society.

If you scored 15–21 points some of the things mentioned in the above category may also apply to you to a degree, specially if your score was nearer 21 than 15.

Generally you are able to disregard too many conventionally based judgements in your personal relationships, and your feelings for someone will not be unduly influenced by your need for social approval.

You are not too worried about what your friends and neighbours think of your relationships. The good and lovable qualities *you* see in your partner are far more important to you than any disapproval of him/her which may come from the outside world. So, compared to the higher scorers in this section you are far more tolerant of your partner's actions and attitudes, far more willing to accept a certain amount of eccentricity or non-conformist behaviour in the other person, and of course this will add to a better understanding of him/her as a person, and in many ways a more relaxed relationship.

You will recognize the other person's need for self-expression and be able to devote your attention to their individual qualities. You can see problems in your relationships more clearly, because you are less likely to pre-judge or to dismiss the emotional factors involved.

If you scored 9–14 points rigidly conventional judgements do not enter into your relationships, and you appreciate the unique qualities of individual character. You do not expect people to fit into conventional patterns, and while you may like to admire socially acceptable traits in people, your admiration stems from your own moral and personal standards rather than the standards laid down by convention. The same principle applies to the qualities in people of which you disapprove and dislike.

You can use your own judgements and conduct your relationships the way you want them. Being unafraid of what others in general think of your relationships, you create a sense of personal freedom in which people can act naturally and be themselves. This is not necessarily an attitude of rebellion against convention, but a need for truth and personal reality in your relationships.

Being largely unhampered by social pressures, you are able to see situations clearly and to understand the personal motives of your partner. You can also be reasonably sure that your demands and expectations are genuine, and that you are forming relationships because of the emotional needs of your personality; because of your own feelings about people rather than their image in the eyes of the world. You will be able to face up to problems in your relationships and try to solve them on an emotional level.

SECTION TWO—FANTASY

Everyone would like to be unconditionally loved and adored. Probably the most common cause of tension and resentment in relationships is simply lack of love: that one or both partners feel they are not getting the love, care and attention they deserve.

The trouble is that unless you are very lucky, the more unconditional love you demand the more disappointed you are likely to be.

Most people have at least a vague fantasy of what a perfect relationship should be, but clinging too desperately to a fantasy and failing to come to terms with the reality of a relationship causes many problems, and often tends only to widen the gap between real feeling and the shining image of ideal love.

If you scored 22–27 points in this section you feel a great need to be loved and admired. You are liable to become hostile in a relationship if your demands are not met; if you feel you are not loved or appreciated enough, perhaps failing to take into account whether your behaviour has been worthy of the love you desire.

There is the danger of wanting to receive love more than you want to give love. In some relationships perhaps the other person will be quite happy about the arrangement and lavish you with love without asking so much back in return, but in general your more excessive demands are more likely to cause conflict than joy. The more the relationship moves away from the perfect image of love, the more dissatisfied you will become; and this will also prevent you from appreciating the good things in the relationship and the good qualities of the other person.

When things go wrong in your relationships you automatically tend to blame the other person. You don't want to see your own imperfections or to admit equal responsibility for failure, so you will convince yourself that it's the other person's fault. And of course if the other person feels that he/she is being unfairly blamed he/she is likely to retaliate by withdrawing the expression of love, and so resentment between you builds up.

One of the problems is that you tend to see the other person too much in relation to yourself; i.e. the way he/she affects your feelings and your self-image, without giving him/her enough credit as a person with a separate life, with thoughts, feelings and interests which are not necessarily bound up with you. This kind of subjective view of people will obstruct your understanding of their feelings and motives, making it more difficult for you to sort out mutual emotional problems.

The thing to come to terms with is that no relationship is entirely perfect, and it's unfair to compare someone with an ideal fantasy—the comparison is bound to be odious. But in real terms, if you can lower your expectations and start from reality your relationships will be much easier to cope with, and probably much more rewarding.

If you scored 15–21 points some of the things mentioned in the above category may also apply to you to a degree, specially if your score was nearer 21 than 15.

In general, although you would like to bring your fantasies into real life, you can accept an existing situation and come to terms with the fact that relationships may not always be perfect. You are prepared to acknowledge that the people close to you also have their own lives to lead and cannot always fulfil your demands of them. But being rather a sensationalist by nature, you tend to feel peeved and discontented when your emotional life lacks drama, and you may be tempted to see your own boredom as a reflection of your partner's failure to provide enough interest and stimulation.

Your egotistical streak, normally fairly well under control, can break out from time to time. You are sensitive even to implied criticism, for instance, so that friendly 'heart to heart' discussions easily become fiery scenes or hurt, resentful silences. However, the more you can build up your own self-esteem the less you will have to rely on your relationships as ego-boosters, and the more room there will be for genuine mutual love and affection. Your fantasy image of love can in fact act as a useful goal in finding happiness as long as it is not too far removed from reality.

If you scored 9–14 points you don't feel that you have an automatic right to be loved, and you can be realistic about your relationships because your fantasy image of love doesn't overshadow reality. For people who are secure about themselves, being loved is very much to be desired, but it is not a desperate need. So there are times when you can lack love from the outside world and still maintain your self-esteem. In other words you don't have to rely on love or admiration as a means of emotional salvation.

Because you don't expect unconditional love from people around you, you are prepared to go at least half way towards building up good relationships, and your demands on those close to you will be comparatively modest and reasonable. You are not likely to make people feel that they have failed you. You will take half the responsibility for failure when things go wrong, and because you are willing to admit equal blame you are less likely to provoke long-term anger and resentment in your partner.

You are able to keep problems and hostilities in perspective, and your inner sense of security enables you to face up to conflicts without losing your basic faith in relationships. You can stand up to reasonable criticism, and you avoid taking things too personally. In avoiding *prima donna* attitudes you can deal sensibly and fairly with others. However involved you may be with someone, you can still see the relationship objectively. Your loving behaviour is motivated by genuine affection and concern for the other person, rather than by self-interest.

SECTION THREE—ADJUSTMENT
Living with other people can often involve many minor annoyances and irritations which are not serious in themselves, but which can build up to a lot of resentment in a relationship.

It's fine to have strong views and opinions, and a well disciplined routine for day-to-day living, but adjustment to other people can be made difficult if you are too set in your ways, too unwilling to make compromises, and too critical of the other person's failure to match up to your standards.

If you scored 22–27 points in this section you tend to have fixed opinions and standards and a very clear idea of how you wish to conduct your life. You also have a clear idea of what you think is right behaviour and what you think is wrong, and your moral judgements can be quite harsh at times. You tend to be critical of people around you, finding it difficult to accept characteristics which are less than perfect.

Your relationships may run into trouble because you are quick to find fault with your partner. Your partner may in turn begin to feel 'got at' and unfairly accused. This kind of situation can develop into a petty war with a great deal of snapping and squabbling. The danger is that small day-to-day hostilities can build up so much that they over-shadow the good and pleasant aspects of the relationship.

As you will tend automatically to put yourself in the right and the other person in the wrong, the circle of hostility will be hard to break once it takes a grip.

In many cases, of course, others will agree with your opinions and live up to your standards, but there are bound to be occasions when a more tolerant and relaxed attitude on your part would save a lot of trouble and bad feeling. You are just as ready to approve of the good qualities you see in people as to disapprove of the bad ones, so if the situation is right you can be happy and at peace with someone.

The trouble is that you are inclined to overreact if the situation is *not* right. You may then lose respect for the other person, reacting only to their faults and being unable to appreciate their virtues. One possible cure for this, perhaps, would be to concentrate less on detail and more on an overall image of someone's personality. For instance instead of thinking of someone as 'that person who tells lies or has disgusting table manners', try to see their personality and situation as a whole, and this may make it easier to forgive faults and make allowances.

If adjustments have to be made in a relationship your idea is that the other person should change their ways to suit *you*, and this might be too much to expect of someone unless you are willing to make compromises too.

If you scored 15–21 points some of the things mentioned in the above category may also apply to you to a degree, specially if your score was nearer 21 than 15.

In general you have strongly but not rigidly held values and although it is your instinct to be critical, you are able to modify your opinions and judgements. You will certainly complain when standards fall too low in your relationships but you can keep a sense of proportion and you are usually willing to listen to the other person's point of view.

You will not make the other person feel they are in the wrong all the time, and with enough flexibility on your part, you are able to accept that other people's standards and priorities are not always the same as yours. In recognizing their differences you can be more tolerant and understanding, rather than automatically picking on their faults and blaming their inadequacies.

When petty irritations build up too much you probably do your share of nagging and snapping, but you don't allow minor hostilities to overrule the more important aspects of the relationship, and you don't allow small quarrels to affect your basic appreciation and affection for the other person.

It is likely that in principle you dislike change, but you are still adaptable enough to compromise and adjust to those around you.

If you scored 9–14 points you are generally easy-going in your relationships, able to accept people as they are and to come to terms with their faults. You are likely to have a lot of personal tolerance, ready to give people the benefit of the doubt and willing to put up with some inconvenience if necessary to maintain harmony.

In the main you reserve your criticisms for important issues, and you can overcome small irritations, so your relationships should be free from petty bickering.

You have enough confidence in yourself not to feel threatened by beliefs and attitudes which are different from your own, and rather than condemning people you will try to understand their views before you judge them.

You do not need to cling to the familiar for security, and being unafraid of change you can adapt easily to new people and situations.

In close relationships you can adjust to your partner's ideas and wishes without losing sight of yourself. You recognize the fact that people have different personalities, that they don't always want the same things and cannot always agree. Usually you can accept this without resentment so that the other people in your life feel they can express themselves and lead their own lives without fear of criticism and disapproval.

SECTION FOUR—CONTROL OF RELATIONSHIPS
In relationships there is ideally a natural balance between acquiescing to the other person's wishes and asserting your own will upon them. Too much aggression will result in battles and conflicts and yet extreme modesty and lack of aggression also bring their own problems.

If you have scored 22–27 points in this section you have a tendency to get carried along in the tide, drifting into relationships without a feeling of having much control over them.

You often fail to be very discriminating about people you choose to mix with, partly because you need the reassurance of their friendship as a shield against loneliness, and partly because you genuinely don't know what you want in life. You have a strong need for the warmth and comfort of friendship and the need itself can sometimes overpower your sense of self-protection and your judgement. This means that you find it difficult to say no to people, and your instincts, often lacking self-criticism, can lead you into unsuitable situations.

Your relationships can sometimes run into trouble because you are not demanding enough in many ways, and you don't make it plain to people how you expect to be treated. Your own laxness or diffidence in this respect may contribute to tension and insecurity in your relationships.

You will certainly be hostile or resentful if you feel you are being taken for granted or under-valued, but it is also up to you to give your partner a guideline of what you expect from him/her. If you don't assert yourself sufficiently in relationships people can sometimes read your over-tolerance as a lack of interest and involvement, and they will then be made to feel confused and insecure. So it is important to show that you care, and not to be afraid of expressing anger, because although it's painful at the time an expression of strong emotion will get your feelings across and show the other person that you're deeply involved and treating the situation seriously.

If you scored 15–21 points some of the things mentioned in the above category may also apply to you up to a point, specially if your score was nearer 21 than 15.

In general you feel you have control over your relationships and you can assert yourself and make your feelings and wishes known.

Basically you have a good idea of what is right and what is wrong for you in a relationship. You are willing to be swayed and influenced sometimes and the extent to which you assert yourself varies depending on how self-confident you feel in the relationship, and how much you need the other person's love and approval at the time.

Sometimes you may find it difficult to share your life with other people without losing any sense of your own identity. Your image of yourself tends to change quite a lot according to the people you are with, and you will tend to pick up their habits and mannerisms. You are aware of social pressures, but can make the effort to withstand them when you want to.

If you scored 9—14 points you have a strong sense of your own identity, knowing who you are and what you want in life. Your basic faith in yourself means that you can control your own life and have the courage of your own convictions.

However involved you are with people you don't lose sight of yourself, and although you may consciously decide to give in to social pressures you are not afraid to rebel occasionally and perhaps risk loneliness or disapproval as a result.

Because you don't depend on people too much for emotional support you can enter into relationships for the right reasons—simply because you like the people you choose as friends and enjoy their company. You can offer genuine friendship, and not needing charity or protection from others, you look for equal relationships.

You can be objective in your judgements of people so you won't very often make mistakes or get yourself involved in situations which become unpleasant or difficult. Having a clear image of your own personality, you are less likely to find yourself acting out of character and then having to cope with the resulting problems.

You have little trouble in being able to assert yourself in relationships, and hopefully you can also bend to the wishes and needs of others sometimes, too.

SECTION FIVE—COMMUNICATION

Lack of communication is one of the most common causes of unhappiness in close relationships. People vary a great deal in their need to communicate with others, and in their ability to express their feelings.

If you scored 22—27 points in this section you are a private person who either cannot or does not need to talk to others very often simply for the sake of communication. You will talk to people when you have something to say or when you find yourself on the right wavelength with someone, but you tend not to use conversation to encourage intimacy and friendship. In fact it's probable that the other person has to go more than half way in making the effort to befriend you.

You don't give your friendship away lightly and you reserve your emotional expressiveness for those whom you know well; for people you have grown to love and trust.

While many of your personal relationships may be deeply satisfying and rewarding, there is a danger that problems may crop up in your relationships through loss of emotional contact. Unless the other person can interest you and involve you totally you tend to 'switch off' and go back into your private world.

Other people are then likely to feel shut out and rejected. Their resentment is made worse because they will find it difficult to understand why they have been given such cold treatment—they haven't committed any sins yet they're still being punished.

If they become hostile you are likely to retreat even more into yourself and if they try to force their emotional demands on you, you will also tend to feel threatened, becoming even more uncommunicative in an attempt to guard yourself from intrusion or attack. These problems can be overcome if another person can learn to respect your privacy, and if you can make the effort to give more of yourself, so that you both meet each other half way.

You tend to have difficulty in sharing, not in a material sense, but in sharing your thoughts and emotions and experiences with someone else.

If you scored 15–21 points some of the comments above might apply to you to a degree, especially if your score was nearer 21 than 15.

You would probably like to be able to make more effort to be socially extraverted and make friends more easily, but your communication problems usually decrease with time and when you get to know people you can express your feelings to them and get on to an emotional wavelength with them.

In general you probably fluctuate a great deal in your ability to communicate with others. When you are feeling expansive and self-confident and the atmosphere is right you can be at ease socially; you can express your emotions and radiate warmth and friendship. At other times your sensitivity to people and social atmospheres may cause you to be reserved and rather chilly when others make emotional overtures.

The introverted side of your nature is often helpful in forming very close, deep relationships, but it also sometimes prevents you from making contacts which could be extremely rewarding.

Given that the situation is right, you want to share your life with other people and to become deeply involved. As long as you make the effort to communicate with people around you, you can still enjoy your own private world without becoming emotionally isolated.

If you scored 9–14 points you find it easy and enjoyable to communicate with people and to express your feelings. Being naturally friendly you have enough interest and self-confidence to approach people without fear of being snubbed. You can create a warm atmosphere which encourages others to respond to you.

Lack of communication with others and the resulting sense of isolation is not likely to be one of your problems.

You are attentive to people and therefore make them feel that you are involved with them and interested in them. Even though your communication with those close to you may not always be on a deeply emotional level, you still bring a feeling of friendliness and togetherness into the relationship.

You are generous with your emotions and you get a lot of satisfaction out of your relationships, out of sharing your life and your experiences with others.

INTERPRETATION QUIZ

Look at each picture and choose the interpretation of the situation or relationship which you feel is most apt.

1.

(c) They look exhausted. Perhaps they are waiting for a train or a boat during a long journey.

(b) They are in some sort of hotel foyer, just milling about, but quite at ease.

(d) The atmosphere is terribly sad, as though a tragedy has happened. Perhaps someone has died.

(a) They are applicants for a job, pacing about as they wait to find out which one of them has been successful.

(d) They are deeply involved in their own thoughts after an intense conversation making important decisions and talking about their future.

(c) The evening is getting late. They seem bored and cannot think of anything more to say to each other.

(a) They are trying to calm down and compose themselves after a heated quarrel.

(b) They are happy and content. They've had dinner and a few drinks and they feel very relaxed in each other's company.

3.

(a) The figure in the foreground is looking around, trying to decide which girl he finds most attractive and wants to approach.

(d) The foreground figure is looking for someone special in the crowd. He cannot see her and is becoming rather agitated.

(b) The foreground figure has just arrived at the party and is making his way over to a group of friends.

(c) The foreground figure stands on his own watching the merriment. He feels rather left out.

(b) The man loves both women equally in different ways. He doesn't want to give either of them up, and the women seem to have accepted the situation.

(d). The man loves one of the women, but he is committed to the other one and feels a deep sense of loyalty to her.

(c) The man is at a loss to know what to do. He cannot decide which of the women he loves the most.

(a) It is a very explosive eternal-triangle. Both women are creating jealous scenes, and the man is trying to control the situation.

(c) She looks strange, not quite real, as though she's going through some kind of spiritual experience.

(d) She has seen her lover and is running towards him.

(b) She is playing and larking about on the beach, perhaps with friends or a group of laughing children.

(a) She is exhilarated, ecstatically happy. She jumps for joy and feels she owns the world.

6.

(b) The lone figure feels quite confident as he goes to join the group.

(d) The lone figure feels uneasy, not knowing whether he will be accepted by the group.

(a) The lone figure is the leader of the group, talking to his followers.

(c) Perhaps the lone figure is on trial. The atmosphere is, very tense and sinister.

(d) Perhaps something will go wrong with the romance, but they both know that whatever happens they will always love each other.

(c) It's a clandestine affair, but there is too much opposition to the match, and it can never work out in the end.

(a) It is a very passionate affair. It will be stormy and heart-rending, but it could deepen into lasting love.

(b) They are very much in love. Each moment together is so happy and perfect that they do not have to think about the future.

8.

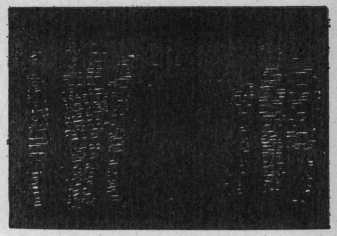

(a) It's like a battleground. There are two rival gangs facing each other. Violence will break out at any moment.

(d) It looks like a primitive ritual ceremony. The boys are on the right and the girls are on the left. They will soon begin a courtship dance.

(b) They have arranged themselves into two teams and are about to engage in some kind of game or sport.

(c) It looks as though the two groups of people are quite separate and do not know each other, yet it seems menacing. One just couldn't tell what is going to happen next.

(b) It is only a temporary parting. They are not too sad because they know they will meet again.

(a) They have chosen separate paths in life and decided to part. There is sadness, but a feeling of hope, too.

(c) She has rejected him. He has taken it well on the surface, but is suffering underneath.

(d) It is very tragic. Their love is hopeless. They have made a suicide pact because they cannot bear to live without each other.

(c) They are in great danger. They are being followed; probably by the secret police.

(a) There has been a disaster, perhaps a plane crash, and they are running to get help for the other survivors.

(d) It is an elopement. They are running away to start a new life together.

(b) They are lost and trying to find their way through the gloom to the nearest village.

(d) It is a reunion of old friends who haven't seen each other for a long time. There is a wonderful atmosphere of warmth and togetherness.

(c) It is quite a pleasant gathering, but somehow the people are too frenetic in their efforts to enjoy themselves—they are overdoing it a bit.

(b) It is just what it seems to be—a happy family celebration perhaps for an engagement or a christening. They'll probably all have hangovers tomorrow, but for the moment they are all very happy.

(a) It is a happy family party on the surface, but they do not know yet that one of the guests has been murdered in the bathroom upstairs.

(b) The situation looks worse than it really is. It is a sort of play-acting quarrel which is not too serious.

(d) It is a serious argument about a very important problem where they are both in conflict. It will take a long time to resolve the problem.

(a) It is a very violent argument, but it will be resolved quickly as soon as one of them gives way.

(c) The quarrel is extremely serious and the problem behind it is more or less insoluble. The two men probably won't want to see each other ever again after this.

(a) They are old, but still energetic and spirited. They don't want to give up any of their interests or ambitions.

(b) They are a contented old couple out for a stroll. They probably live in a cottage not far away.

(c) They are trying to find food and shelter. They are poor and homeless and no-one cares about them.

(d) They are setting out on a last, symbolic journey of some kind; perhaps to revisit their native land and rejoin their relatives for their remaining days.

Now count your score, mainly (a) (b) (c) or (d) and turn to the CONCLUSIONS.

CONCLUSIONS

The Interpretation Quiz aimed to find out what your expectations of people are: whether you expect people to be friendly, honest, kind, hostile, approachable, scornful and so on.

These expectations are partly a result of your personality, which will determine the way you react to people, and partly a result of your previous experience of people. As you go through life an opinion of people in general builds up in your mind, and may well change quite radically as your circumstances change. For instance when you are happily in love with someone, your feelings of beauty and tenderness caste a rosy glow over the whole human race; *everyone* seems nicer, lovelier; in the same way that when you're going through a lot of stress and conflict in your relationships, your view of the whole human race tends to be tinged with grey.

You usually have a vague idea of what people are like, even before you meet them or know them properly. Your expectations of them will influence the way you react to them, and the way you get on with them.

Mostly (a)

You expect relationships to be dramatic and difficult, and there nearly always seems to be an element of competitiveness in your interaction with people, even though it is often hidden beneath the surface.

You recognize the cruel and evil side of human nature and are able to come to terms with it and stand up to it if necessary. Because you are aware of the darker side of people's motives, you are prepared for all eventualities, you are ready to cope with difficult situations.

Although you don't automatically expect people to be kind, charming and beautiful, you are not bitter or disillusioned. You anticipate problems, but there is also a powerful feeling that problems can be solved, that despite everything there is hope. You have faith that you can overcome opposition, and if relationships are sometimes a battle, you have confidence that you can win.

You feel you have the power to make or break relationships; you want to exert influence and to be admired by those around you.

You become rebellious when under stress, you cannot tolerate frustration of any kind, and your strong feelings can sometimes cause a certain recklessness in your relationships. You expect others to have the same strong, forceful feelings, and can sometimes be scornful of those who are content to live on a lower plane of emotional activity.

You want to be intensely involved with people, but part of you often refuses to be too committed. You appear to be spontaneous and impulsive in your dealings with people, but you can also be calculating, summing up the other person, weighing up the situation; so you have a hard centre which is alert to danger and ready to spring to attack when you feel threatened.

A certain amount of tension is essential in your relationships if you are to remain interested, and a certain level of drama and complication is also a welcome source of stimulation.

You look for people who are equal or above your level in some way. You want to learn from them. If you admire someone you want to find out more about them, to observe how they operate and if possible to make their attributes your own, and hopefully to surpass them. Ambitious and determined, you seek information from others, and you are interested in any ideas or attitudes which may expand your own horizons and stretch your own abilities.

Basically you feel that people have a tremendous amount to offer and that you can enrich your own experience of life through them. You can often become overstimulated by people. There is a basic feeling of self-confidence in your attitude to others, an optimistic strength of purpose. Whatever the difficulties are you expect things to work out right in the end and you know that you can cope.

Mainly (b)

You have a very optimistic view of social relationships. You expect people to be friendly and co—operative, you expect them to trust you and react warmly to you and you can therefore approach others with confidence and break through many social barriers which are closed to the more socially sensitive and diffident.

Having a rational view of people, you realize that people are human whatever their position, their circumstances or life-styles and you can always relate to them simply as human beings with feelings, problems and desires in common with your own. People present no threat to you, and any opportunity for affiliation and companionship will be welcome to you.

You have a feeling of genuine good will towards people and you expect this feeling to be returned. You can be open and defenceless, relaxed with people and able to express yourself freely. Your expectations of people are good. In other words you are willing to believe people are good until you are proved wrong.

You are socially active, and you look for easy-going communication, fun and stimulation. The enjoyment and laughter to be gained from relationships is very important for you. You have the ability to blend with others, to share your pleasures with them and lose yourself in the communal spirit of the occasion. There is often a kind of relaxed joyfulness in your relationships.

The fun of the moment in relationships is more important than the future development of the friendship; so you may sometimes 'run through' people rather fast. Your emotional reactions to people are immediate and impulsive; you can accept people easily and overlook their faults; you want to be genuinely popular and you are usually prepared to like and approve of people instantly.

Perhaps you are rather self-indulgent sometimes in your motivation towards the gratification of your senses and desires. You are easily attracted to people, both sexually and for sensual warmth which is not necessarily connected with sex. Body language, body contact with people is an essential and natural part of your communication with them; from sexual contact to putting your arm round a friend, standing close to someone or staring into their eyes as you talk to them. This kind of warm physical intimacy is very pleasurable and satisfying to you, but the deeper aspects of a relationship may sometimes be neglected. Because you look for immediate gratification you may not always be prepared to put a lot of long-term effort into relationships.

With the expectation that relationships are going to be straightforward and problem-free, you attach yourself to people readily and easily. When relationships are running smoothly you will be content to stay and expend your warmth and generosity of spirit, but your sense of commitment may vanish when problems arise and the element of ease and enjoyment is lost.

Mainly (c)
You tend to be rather pessimistic in your attitude towards relationships in general. There is sometimes a feeling of gloom and despondency that things are too difficult, that understanding cannot be reached, that you will be obstructed in trying to get what you want from relationships.

Other people often seem to be remote and mysterious creatures. It is difficult to understand their motives or to find an emotional affinity with them, to know how to relate to them in a way which is meaningful and genuine. You go through moods and times when you feel people do not appreciate you; when the world in general has let you down and there doesn't seem to be anyone to rely on. There may be a feeling of detachment and futility in your dealings with others, as though you are simply going through the motions of communication, but without any real emotional contact.

During these bleak moments you wish you could bridge the gap of feeling between yourself and others, but your expectation of stress in relationships tends to increase, and you are easily put off, easily discouraged. You may feel it is less painful to remain self-contained and uncommitted, shielding yourself from the dangers of involvement with people and yet yearning for friendship in the deepest sense.

Depressive bouts cause you to be self-willed and yet over-sensitive to the reactions of others. People seem threatening or forbidding; there seem to be few opportunities for emotional fulfilment; people seem unrewarding, unable to offer you anything, and you feel you cannot trust them enough to risk friendship and intimacy in case of rejection and humiliation. You find it hard to believe that relationships will ever work out, or lead to anything good.

In a sense relationships are *too* important to you. There is too much at stake, so you are often unable to approach people casually and easily. There is a great deal of conflicting thought and feeling inside you, and you tend to see relationships as being far more difficult and complicated than they really are. Because your feelings are so intense you tend to over-estimate the intensity of other people's feelings.

However, in brighter moods when you are not depressed your attitude towards people can change quite radically.

Being sensitive to people, you are highly stimulated by social encounters and a warm or fascinating and interesting conversation with someone can leave an after-glow, making the whole world suddenly feel brighter and more beautiful.

You seek real communication with others and when you can trust people and feel a sense of rapport with them you will value the relationship a great deal. You are able to find emotional satisfaction in close relationships.

Basically you look for people of your own kind, people with the same depth of feeling and insight; people who are able to communicate on your level. You want allies;

people who are 'on your side', who understand and sympathize with your views and who recognize the special, personal qualities which you feel can only really be appreciated by people who know you well. Like-minded friends will reassure you that you are not alone in your views and beliefs, and that your feelings and values in life are good and worthwhile.

Mainly (d)

You expect relationships to be deeply emotional with a certain undercurrent of melodrama. In your idealized view circumstances are powerful and eventful, often tragic and hopeless, yet your people are irrevocably tied together and passionately involved with each other. Their feelings are searing and noble and extremely romantic.

This echoes your need for a strong emotional element in your relationships. You want to experience extremes of feeling, to stretch out every moment of emotion and sentiment, to dramatize situations and events. You want to expand your experience of life through relationships and you have high expectations of people.

There is a feeling of searching. Perhaps you are searching for some quality you lack, or for some deeper meaning and purpose in life which you hope to find through your relationships with others.

Your quest is for a kind of aesthetic sensitivity and emotional unity. You want to identify very closely with people and achieve perfect understanding, but you do not want to make your desires too obvious. You long for thrilling and unusual things to happen to you, and for relationships of extraordinary intensity. It is likely you realize that you tend to be over-imaginative in your expectations, so you will try to hide your feelings for fear of being rebuffed or thought silly. Your feelings will often cause you embarrassment.

Despite your desire for deep affinity with others you will often be reserved and cautious with people, because you do not want to be caught out or 'seen through'.

You realize that people cannot always offer the depth of sympathy and understanding you require.

Sometimes you are disappointed by the lack of sensitivity in others and you feel you are not getting your share of love and attention. Relationships seem routine and uninspiring and there is a sense of waste, as though wonderful, loving qualities in you are mouldering away, unable to find expression.

At other times you feel that emotional fulfilment is very near achievement, and there is a sense of nervous anticipation.

Close relationships, which are taken extremely seriously, enable you to gratify many of your desires. You feel the need to analyze relationships, to nurture them and keep a careful watch over them. Even when you are very happy and satisfied there is an underlying sense of anxiety. Your joy in relationships is so important and valuable that you fear loss of happiness. Even when things are near-perfect, they are not quite perfect enough, and instead of a total enjoyment of the moment you will be one or two steps ahead, worrying about the future. When people respond to you it is somehow 'too good to last', when they don't respond to you it is a lonely and bitterly disappointing experience. So you make a lot of your feelings; tending to build them up into melodramas of ecstasy or tragedy.

MARRIAGE QUIZ

What do you see in each other?

The Marriage Quiz is composed of two separate quizzes, one for the wife and one for the husband.

The conclusions will give you an indication of what you see in each other and what you want from the relationship; how closely your attitudes towards marriage match up with each other, and which needs or ideals, if any, are not being sufficiently fulfilled by each other.

QUIZ FOR WIFE

1. When he cuts his finger, what do you do?
   - (c) You get the plaster and ask if he needs any help.
   - (a) You know he can cope with it by himself.
   - (b) You sit him down and act as nurse.

2. When he does the washing up for you, are you—
   - (a) very surprised?
   - (c) just glad you don't have to do it yourself?
   - (b) very appreciative indeed, and perhaps even slightly guilty about letting him do it?

3. If he introduced you to his new boss, do you think you would be—
   - (c) quite light-hearted about it, slightly seductive, maybe?
   - (b) friendly, but sum him up in your mind?
   - (a) very charming, but rather diffident?

4. When he's going through a particularly difficult time at work, do you—
   - (b) make his home life specially calm and comfortable?
   - (a) wait until he wants to tell you about it?
   - (c) get him to talk about it as soon as possible?

5. When he tells you off about something, do you usually—
   - (a) apologize?
   - (c) justify yourself heatedly?
   - (b) explain quite calmly why you did it?

6. How do you usually plan a joint social outing?
    (b) You usually make the arrangements.
    (a) He usually makes the arrangements.
    (c) Neither of you does particularly more planning or arranging than the other.

7. If he were to acquire a very glamorous new secretary or work-mate, would you—
    (a) feel a bit uneasy, but say nothing?
    (c) question him about his feelings towards her?
    (b) tease him about her?

8. When you are the only woman with your husband and a crowd of his male friends, do you feel—
    (c) completely natural and not specially conscious of being the only woman?
    (b) rather amused by them all?
    (a) a bit self-conscious and left out?

9. How do you react when he talks about his work?
    (b) You feel you are a sympathetic listener.
    (a) You try, but find it hard to visualize exactly what his problems are.
    (c) You are genuinely interested.

10. If he forgot to buy you a birthday present, would you—
    (a) forgive him, but be quietly hurt and upset?
    (c) be noisily furious?
    (b) be really very good-natured and understanding about it?

Count your score, mainly (a) (b) or (c) and turn to
CONCLUSIONS FOR WIFE.

QUIZ FOR HUSBAND

1. When does your wife look nicest to you—
   - (a) in her old clothes.
   - (c) when she's all dressed up.
   - (b) in good casual clothes.

2. When you're feeling ill, do you—
   - (c) enjoy sympathy but refrain from acting too sick?
   - (a) make a fuss?
   - (b) suffer bravely in silence?

3. When she has a row with a shopkeeper, or a similar difficulty, do you—
   - (b) take up the battle on her behalf?
   - (c) advise her what her next step should be?
   - (a) keep well out of it?

4. How do you react when your wife mends a fuse or does some difficult practical task around the house?
   - (a) You appreciate it and feel pleased that she is capable of doing practical tasks.
   - (b) You tend to overdo the glowing praise rather.
   - (c) Beyond noticing the repair, or whatever, you don't give it any more thought.

5. When you are going through a particularly difficult time at work, do you tend to—
   - (a) ask your wife's advice about it?
   - (c) describe the situation and complain to her about it?
   - (b) refrain from mentioning it to her unless it gets really bad?

6. When you feel your wife is being unreasonable, being over-critical and starting a scene or quarrel, are you most likely to—
   - (c) fly into a rage?
   - (b) defend yourself verbally, but refuse to get heated until you are provoked too far?
   - (a) storm out of the room rather than prolonging the argument/sulk?

7. If your wife burnt the dinner, or a similar minor disaster, how are you likely to react?
   (a) You'd be irritated/annoyed/upset.
   (c) You'd probably laugh about it and make fun of her.
   (b) You'd comfort her and tell her it doesn't matter.
8. How would you react if your wife flirted rather too much with someone at a party?
   (c) You'd be angry and jealous on the spot.
   (a) You'd tell her off about it afterwards.
   (b) You would be unworried about it.
9. How do you react to boring, unpleasant chores/repairs around the house?
   (a) You tend to leave them undone.
   (c) You get round to doing them, but usually fuss or get bad-tempered over them.
   (b) You do them more or less immediately with no fuss or bother.
10. At a formal or office party, do you tend to—
    (c) talk to men and women more or less equally?
    (b) talk mostly to other men?
    (a) talk mostly to women?

Count your score, mainly (a) (b) or (c) and turn to CONCLUSIONS FOR HUSBAND.

CONCLUSIONS FOR WIFE

Mostly (a)

You see your marriage very much in traditional terms, where the roles of the husband and wife are clearly defined.

Apart from seeing your husband as a friend and lover, you see him as a figure of authority, and his dominion in the home gives you the emotional security you need. You want to be able to rely on him, to trust his judgement, and to feel that you know where you are with him, so his predictability as a man and as a husband is important to you; his unwavering sense of responsibility and of 'rightness' is reassuring to you.

You admire male qualities of strength and self-confidence, which may have been the qualities you looked up to in your own father, or perhaps the admirable qualities associated with manliness which you have been brought up to respect. You tend to be attracted to all the characteristics which go with the archetypal image of manhood —pride, courage, ambition, self-assertion, and so on.

You want to be able to respect your husband's position as a provider, and also as a guide and mentor. If you yourself tend to lack confidence, to be uncertain or confused about your values and aims, your husband's decided emotions and fixed views will compensate for your doubts and give you a great deal of comfort.

Your husband probably has a high standard in his expectations of what a wife should be, and if you enjoy living up to his standards you should be very happy.

Ideally your husband should have answered (b) in his Quiz. This means that he accepts and enjoys the traditional male role in marriage, he likes to feel needed, to feel he is in charge and to know that you appreciate his strength of character and his achievements. He wants to protect you as much as you want to be protected. Your very feminine attitude towards him enhances his own pride in being masculine.

If your husband answered mainly (a) in his Quiz it is possible that the responsibility of the marriage sometimes weighs heavily on him. Like you, he needs and appreciates emotional closeness and togetherness in the relationship, but he doesn't always want the responsibility of being the decision-maker; he'd like you to share commitments more and to rely on him rather less. Perhaps he feels you don't always understand that *he* sometimes needs help, encouragement and moral support, too.

If your husband answered mainly (c) in his Quiz, he sometimes wishes you would assert yourself more. He appreciates you for your qualities as an individual rather than just as a wife, and the traditional ideals of marriage are less important to him than they are to you. The more you develop your own personality and interests the more he will admire and respect you.

Mostly (b)

You see your marriage in fairly traditional terms as a close, supportive relationship, and as a serious commitment.

You have a highly developed maternal instinct and apart from seeing your husband as a friend and lover you also see him as someome who needs all the wifely loving care you can give him. The more little-boy qualities he has the more you will want to look after him, especially in a practical way.

You are realistic and gentle, and you have the instinct of a home-maker, being concerned about creating a good environment and enjoying responsibility, getting a lot of satisfaction from the feeling that your husband and other members of your family are depending on you. You enjoy making decisions and organizing home life, and although you respect your husband's judgements you feel it is your duty to take over the practical running of the marriage. Perhaps you feel that by taking charge of your joint domestic life you can free your husband from irksome chores and enable him to devote himself to the things which are really important to him.

You are generous-hearted with the instinctive desire to give, to provide, to comfort and protect. If these instincts are satisfied and fulfilled in your marriage you should be very happy.

It is important for you to know that your husband wants the love you need to give. If he relies on you and appreciates your capabilities your self-confidence will be enhanced both as a woman and as a person. You will gain a basic sense of worth and pleasure in your marriage.

If your husband answered mainly (a) in his Quiz it means that he does indeed appreciate all your good qualities, and he does need the love you give him. Your commitment to him and to the marriage gives him a great sense of harmony and security. Perhaps he sometimes appears to take you for granted because he is very sure of your love for him. You are so much a natural part of his life that he doesn't have to question the relationship.

If your husband answered mainly (b) in his Quiz he will certainly be proud of your capabilities as a wife and homemaker, and he will appreciate the very female aspects of your personality. The only danger is that, having very definite ideas about his own masculinity, he may see your loving concern as a bid to manage or dominate him. He very definitely wants to see himself as the stronger partner and he wants your admiration rather than your protection. He may wish you to be just a bit more vulnerable and reliant on him.

If your husband answered mainly (c) in his Quiz he appreciates your love, but may wish to communicate with you on a more emotional level. Being a non-conformist he wants to see the partnership primarily as a *relationship* and only secondarily as a marriage of traditional roles. He may sometimes resent your concern for him, misinterpreting it as interference. Although he may enjoy the material comfort you provide, his interest in you and love for you are evoked by your qualities as a person rather than as a wife.

Mostly (c)

You have a modern approach to marriage, seeing it ideally as a union of two people who enjoy being together rather than two people held together by legal ties and traditional principles.

You see your husband as a friend and a lover. You want him to share your beliefs that the marriage should be based on a mutual respect for each other's individuality, and that there should be enough space and freedom in the relationship to allow you both to express yourselves and develop your separate personalities.

You dislike routine and predictability in marriage, and although you can probably cope with domestic life and the responsibilities of being a housewife and mother, you need very much more in life to gain a sense of reward and fulfilment.

You want your husband and family to see you as a person with your own very definite identity; an identity which can be incorporated into the home and into all aspects of your family life. You certainly want a close relationship with your husband, and where possible you will become involved in his life and take on many of his interests—but never simply for the sake of togetherness and never at the expense of your own aims and interests. In fact you will probably bitterly resent cutting down on any of your interests and you will try very hard to keep them going and combine them with the demands of marriage.

It is important for you to be able to love and respect your husband for himself, for what he is rather than what he does, for his personality rather than his position in society or his achievements. The emotional quality of the relationship and the depth of communication between you are all-important.

If your husband answered mainly (c) in his Quiz, he is in agreement with your beliefs and ideals, accepting you as an equal and a fellow-traveller through life. He appreciates the fact that you are on the same emotional wavelength and he respects your views and feelings. Because you have both dismissed traditional guidelines for marriage, the relationship may sometimes be stormy, but your husband has enough faith in you as a person to know that conflicts can be overcome, and emotional traumas can be forgiven and forgotten. The important thing is that he doesn't feel restricted or held back by the relationship.

If your husband answered mainly (a) in his Quiz he may disapprove of many of your views about freedom within marriage, and he may feel justified in demanding that you take the practicalities of home life more seriously and look after his interests more. Although he admires your strength of character and individuality he needs more support from you, more comfort and sympathy perhaps. He is more committed to the traditional ideal of marriage than you are and therefore wishes you could be rather more wifely.

If your husband answered mainly (b) he probably finds it hard to come to terms with the fact that you want to be an equal partner in the marriage. He believes in the traditional male role of domination and may see your independent spirit as an act of rebellion against him. He will certainly see you as a challenge and is not likely to give up his attempt to 'tame' you easily.

CONCLUSIONS FOR HUSBAND

Mostly (a)

You have a traditional view of marriage, seeking a close, trusting relationship and domestic harmony. Home life is ideally a haven for you, peaceful and relaxed.

You see your wife as the provider of this harmonious environment. You appreciate the womanly qualities of warmth, gentleness and kindness, and if your wife possesses these qualities you will be very happy.

You want your wife to take on most of the responsibilities of the home. As you are probably not very practical you like to feel that your wife can deal with day-to-day decisions and cope with some of the irksome chores and the routine planning and organization of your lives.

You need the security of a well run home life and a secure and loving marriage as a background from which you can go out and tackle the world. If your wife provides the comfort you need and if the maternal side of her nature is fulfilled in looking after your interests, you should be a very well matched couple.

You want to be able to admire your wife as a person, for her strength and certainty about life, for her sensible outlook and cheerful attitudes.

You look for a deep sense of unity and belonging; a sense of implicit faith in the relationship, so constancy and loyalty are all-important.

If your wife answered mainly (b) in her Quiz, her ideal of marriage matches yours. She sees the marriage as a union of two people who are completely committed to each other. She has a strong protective instinct and she enjoys the feeling that she is making people happy and creating a secure environment for her family. She will therefore gain a sense of pleasure and pride in the fact that you need what she has to offer, and that you appreciate her as a woman and wife as well as a person in her own right.

If your wife answered mainly (a) in her Quiz, it is likely that although she shares many of your emotional attitudes towards marriage in the traditional sense, she needs more guidance and moral support from you. She would probably like you to take a more active part in home life and to relieve her of some of the chores and responsibilities. Being very feminine and sometimes insecure and uncertain of her own judgements and abilities, she would like to be able to rely on your help and encouragement; and to feel that you are willing to share her problems and burdens.

If your wife answered mainly (c) in her Quiz it is likely

that although she loves and respects you she doesn't always find it easy to accept your demands. She wants to see herself firstly as a person and secondly as a wife, so she will resent giving up any of her own wishes and interests. She would probably like the relationship to be less traditional and more easy-going in the sense of sharing chores and having more flexible domestic arrangements. This would give her more freedom to pursue her own interests as well as fulfilling her role as a wife.

Mostly (*b*)
You believe in the traditional ideal of marriage, and wish to take on the role as the dominant man. You gain satisfaction from being the provider, from making decisions and feeling that you are in control of your household. You have a strong protective instinct and enjoy fulfilling the needs of your family, and feeling that they are largely dependent on you for their welfare and well-being.

You see your wife in the traditional female role as someone who relies on you and looks up to you. Ideally she should admire you for your strength of character, your sound judgements and capabilities, and also for your achievements and status in the outside world. You enjoy taking responsibility and being appreciated for it, and you draw strength and self-confidence from your wife's trust in you, and her approval of you.

As long as your authority is not threatened, you can be loving and easy-going, but because you have a very definite and rather inflexible view of your position in the home, you will also have definite ideas about what you expect from your wife, and you will expect her to endorse your opinions and live up to your standards.

You look for feminine qualities in your wife: compliance, gentleness and soft-heartedness. If she is also sometimes vulnerable, illogical and rather scatterbrained, you will feel especially warm and protective.

If your wife answered mainly (a) her ideals of marriage

match yours. She needs your strength and protection and is happy to allow you the position of power in the relationship. In fact she both welcomes and admires your dominant qualities. You give her the sense of love and security which is essential to her happiness, and she can be proud of you as a man and a husband. You complement each other's needs and live up to each other's ideals.

If your wife answered mainly (b) it is likely that although she shares many of your convictions about marriage, she may feel that she is not given enough of a share in planning your future and making important decisions. She would like you to take her views more seriously, and she would like to feel that you need her more and depend on her more.

If your wife answered mainly (c) her ideas about marriage are likely to be rather different from yours and she may find it difficult to meet some of your demands, and live up to some of your expectations. Her independence of spirit is very important to her, and she wants to be appreciated more for her qualities and talents as an individual, and less for her role as a wife in the conventional sense. Although she admires your strength, she probably feels that you are inclined to patronize her. She wants to feel loved but not too protected.

Mostly (c)
You don't believe in the traditional ideal of marriage where the male/female roles are sharply divided. You look for a more flexible relationship in marriage, where although closeness and sharing are important you can both keep a sense of separate identity, and you both have enough individual freedom to develop your own personalities and follow your own interests.

You see your wife as an equal; you don't judge her by conventional standards, but admire her for her individual personality and her mental qualities, which make her the person she is.

You see her as a friend and lover rather than as a wife in the conventional sense, and you expect her to contribute as much as you do to the relationship. As there is no laid-down pattern of how you believe a marriage should be conducted, you should both ideally work towards an understanding, and towards building up a life-style which is in tune with both your personalities.

You believe in expressing your emotions, both good and bad, so your wife should have enough self-confidence and enough faith in you to withstand quarrels and conflicts.

You want your wife to be interesting and stimulating as a person; someone who thinks for herself, who is honest in expressing her feelings and confident in her own judgements and opinions.

The ideal is that your love should be based on genuine appreciation for each other, rather than dependence on each other.

If your wife answered mainly (c) she shares your ideas about marriage, being impatient with conventional standards and seeking a freer kind of relationship. She can enjoy being your wife and being *herself*, too; so that although she has to make some concessions and compromises for the sake of the relationship, she doesn't feel diminished as a person.

If your wife answered mainly (a) in her Quiz, she admires your principles and your individual approach to life, but it is likely that she finds it difficult to discard some of her more conventional and traditional ideals of marriage. She may sometimes feel insecure in the relationship and wonder what is expected of her. She would probably like more direction from you, more help and encouragement with day-to-day problems and practical decisions.

If your wife answered mainly (b) in her Quiz she is likely to be very tolerant about your feelings and views about life. Being very warm-hearted and an enthusiastic home-maker she will enjoy taking over the practicalities of the home and marriage so that you can devote yourself to higher objectives. However, she probably wishes you would be rather more involved in day-to-day home life, and she'd like to be more appreciated for her woman's role in the home and in the relationship in general.

PARENTS' QUIZ

The questions in the Parents' Quiz are geared mainly to young children, but if you have older children or no children yet, you can still answer the quiz.

Just think back to your children's younger days, or in the latter case imagine that you already have children and try to gauge how you would respond to the questions asked.

There are no right or wrong answers in this quiz. People have different priorities, different attitudes to child-raising, different emotional reactions. The various methods of bringing up children have their own special advantages, and they can all be equally successful.

1. In the course of day-to-day chat with small children, do you correct their grammar and errors in speech—
   (a) frequently?
   (b) not very often—you usually let it pass?
2. In the general upbringing of children, do you—
   (a) have firm ideas and beliefs?
   (b) tend to 'play it by ear'?
3. How do you feel about the principle of spending a lot of money on a really superb present for a small child?
   (a) It's unnecessary, and not really good for the child, either.
   (b) It's lovely, and gives a lot of pleasure both to the child and to the generous parent.
4. If your small child started learning a musical instrument, would you—
   (a) persuade him/her to practise and organize a regular time each day for it.
   (b) more or less let him/her practise when he/she wants to, but try some gentle persuasion?
5. How do you feel about children brought up under kind but rigid discipline, i.e. the stricter boarding schools, strict religious establishments, etc.?

(a) It needn't be bad—it may give them something 'extra' in life and be a good training for them eventually.

(b) It seems very sad—they are missing out on their childhood.

6. Which do you think is the best reasoning behind letting children have their own pet animals?

(a) It teaches them to be responsible for something smaller than themselves.

(b) It gives them emotional security—love and affection for animals is something very important in their lives.

7. What is your attitude to children's television-watching and comic-reading?

(a) You try to discourage them and limit them as much as possible.

(b) You're quite easy-going about it.

8. If your small child is in difficulty but not in danger, i.e. he's stuck on the first rung of a ladder on the grass, would you—

(a) make suggestions to see if he can deal with the situation himself before picking him up?

(b) rush to pick him up immediately?

9. Are your school holiday/weekend outings most likely to be—

(a) museum visits, wild-life nature films?

(b) funfair, cartoon films?

10. When your small child asks a difficult or abstract question, do you usually—

(a) give a fairly complicated reply in adult terms even though the child might not grasp all of it?

(b) give an over-simplified explanation, which might not always be strictly correct but will be understood by the child?

11. When you are participating in a lively game with young children and they become riotous and over-excited—shrieking, yelling, hysterical laughter, etc. how do you react?

(a) You suddenly cease to be amused, realize the game has gone too far and make efforts to control it and calm everyone down.

(b) You realize the game has got a bit out of hand, but everyone is enjoying it so much that you feel loath to spoil the fun.

Mostly (a)—Go on to SECTION A.
Mostly (b)—Miss SECTION A and go on to SECTION B.

SECTION A

1. When your child has a minor upset or quarrel with a teacher at school, would you—
   (a) tell the child you're sure the teacher knows best and is not being unfair?
   (b) be willing to agree that perhaps the teacher was unfair, and advise the child on what courses of action he/she can take?

2. How seriously do you take disobedience?
   (a) Very seriously on principle.
   (b) Not too seriously if the dispute in question is not very important.

3. Which do you think is a parent's most important duty to prepare an under-five-year-old for starting school?
   (a) To make sure the child is reasonably self-reliant—able to cross roads, be sensible with money, tie shoelaces, etc.
   (b) To make sure he/she knows the alphabet and a few simple words and sums.

4. When a child is very nervous about something—going to the dentist, for instance—how would you react?
   (a) You'd be sympathetic but not make too much fuss about it—tell the child to be brave.
   (b) You'd try to talk the child out of his fear—say

what the dentist will do, reassure him/her that it won't be so bad, etc.

5. When a child (who has private weekly music lessons) is being very awkward and refusing to practise, would you be most inclined to—
   (a) threaten to stop the lessons if he/she doesn't practise (and mean it)?
   (b) threaten to stop the lessons (but not *really* mean it, in the hope that the child will regain enthusiasm) or alternatively not threaten at all?

6. When a small child breaks a clock to 'see what's inside it' do you see it as—
   (a) destructiveness?
   (b) natural childish curiosity?

7. Which statement is true of you?
   (a) You always try to make sure the children are neat, clean and well-dressed.
   (b) You tend not to be very fussy about their appearance on the whole.

8. Which statement applies to you?
   (a) You *always* keep small promises you have made to your children.
   (b) You quite often forget small promises or find you are too busy to carry them out.

9. If your young child gets into mischief with a friend whom you think is a very bad influence, would you—
   (a) forbid your child to see the offending friend again?
   (b) let your child see the friend, but keep a tight watch on them?

10. Do you overdo praise for your young child's painting/drawing/poem, etc. just to encourage him/her to carry on being creative, even when you know the painting, etc. is not really up to the usual standard?
    (a) No.
    (b) Yes, sometimes.

11. Which statement applies to you?

    (a) You feel embarrassed or ashamed if your children see you in tears/in an emotionally overwrought state/in an undignified situation.

    (b) You don't mind the children seeing your weaknesses sometimes.

Mostly (a)—See CONCLUSION ONE.
Mostly (b)—See CONCLUSION TWO.

SECTION B

1. When you take your young children to the pantomime or circus, do you—
   (a) enjoy the experience *through* the children, because of their pleasure and laughter?
   (b) find yourself enjoying the entertainment for yourself as well as for the children?

2. How conscientious are you about taking the children for regular medical/dental check-ups, etc.?
   (a) You are very conscientious.
   (b) You're not always very conscientious.

3. When you have a complaint to make to a teacher at your child's school, do you feel—
   (a) quite confident that you are right to complain?
   (b) rather diffident about it, and not quite sure whether you might be making too much fuss for nothing?

4. When your small child makes a very clever, adult remark, is your first reaction—
   (a) to be very amused?
   (b) to be very impressed?

5. When your young child is rude to you or makes a nasty remark, what is your reaction?
   (a) You're not too upset because you know it's only a temper outburst, and he doesn't really mean it.
   (b) You tend to be personally upset by it.

6. How much do you think you worry in comparison with other parents about the hazards of traffic,

lonely places and other dangers which face young children?

(a) You think you worry more than most parents, because you notice other people often allow their children more physical freedom than you do at an earlier age.

(b) You think you worry about the same amount as other parents.

7. In general do you try to hide your own moods, worries and problems from the children?

(a) Yes. You don't want to burden them with your own troubles.

(b) No. You quite often confide in them about your own problems and feelings.

8. In a toyshop when you are buying a present for a child do you—

(a) look around consciously working out what the child would like most?

(b) often get carried away and buy something *you* think is irresistible and therefore you're sure the child will like it, too?

9. How do you react when a small child says he hates school after the first few days and is very unhappy and scared?

(a) You feel very sorry for the child, but you don't take it to heart too much, being sure he/she will soon settle down.

(b) You tend to become emotionally involved in the child's unhappiness and you feel very wretched about the situation.

10. Imagine your young child has a cold and may be 'sickening for something'. You know you should keep him at home to be on the safe side, yet he/she is keen to go to a friend's party. Would you—

(a) very reluctantly tuck him/her up in bed instead of taking him to the party?

(b) risk it and take him/her to the party?

11. When a child consistently whines and 'niggles', do you feel—
    (a) that you are quite good at remaining patient?
    (b) you lose patience very quickly?

Mostly (a)—See CONCLUSION THREE.
Mostly (b)—See CONCLUSION FOUR.

CONCLUSION ONE

You are a strong parent with a good deal of self-confidence in your own ability to bring up children. Your integrity and sense of certainty in your dealings with your children will give them security, for they know where they are with you, and they also know what is expected of them.

In general you have high expectations of them, and you demand good standards from them.

You treat the business of parenthood very seriously. You have a clear-cut image in your mind of what sort of people you want your children to be; and your upbringing of them is geared to this end. You look to the future and you feel it is your responsibility to train your children; to nurture qualities and attitudes which will be useful to them later in their lives.

You know they will go out into a tough, competitive world and you want to equip them to cope with it. You want them to be morally strong and courageous, to be hard-working and honest, self-disciplined, able to look after themselves and compassionate to others. Perhaps you give them the benefit of a religious faith, but in any case you will teach them a firm moral code which you hope will be with them all their lives and give them something to fall back on.

You are willing to put a great deal of effort into the care and training of your children, and in return you expect results. They will know very definitely when they have pleased you and when they have displeased you, and even though they may feel your judgements are rather harsh at times, they will realize eventually that you have given them something very important—a goal to aim for in life, and a principle to live up to. As long as the power you have over your children is not too dominating or inflexible, they are likely to be very happy and secure. You encourage them to take a pride in themselves, and to recognize and appreciate their own genuine achievements. Although you criticize their faults and failings, you also praise their good qualities and their triumphs, so this should give them a balanced and self-confident view of themselves.

You want your children to be worthy of you, and you try to be worthy of them. You tend to see them as a reflection of yourself and of your image as a parent, so you will be very disappointed when they fail, and very proud when they succeed.

Bringing up children is a very important and very rewarding task. You have faith in your children, and in the love and guidance you can give them, but you may well find the teenage stage very hard to take. If teenagers rebel against you too much, and if they are as strong-willed as you are, a great deal of conflict will result. You will find it extremely hard to understand; and you will find it even harder to give way, to relinquish your power and influence or to compromise on your principles. So this may be a time of difficult adjustment both for you and for your children.

You see yourself very much in the role of a parent and provider, and you want to feel you have given your children every possible advantage for a good start in life.

CONCLUSION TWO

You see children as potential adults, and you are concerned with their whole personalities, and the development of their abilities and talents. Although it is important that they should pass exams and choose good careers, you above all want them to be complete people—happy, self-confident and fulfilled in whatever they choose to do in life.

You aim to bring them up with enough freedom to develop their individuality, but also with enough training and guidance to enable them to make the best of themselves.

You do not want to be seen to be 'pushing' them or inflicting too much discipline. You hope to achieve your objective through gentle encouragement, through providing a stimulating home background and setting an example. If you share your interests and enthusiasms with the children learning becomes a constant and natural part of their everyday lives. You strongly believe that the home as well as the school should be a place of education and mental fascination.

It is likely that you will keep track of their school grades, and take an active part in their school lives, perhaps by offering to help the teachers in any way you can, or by joining school committees. You naturally wish to become involved in all aspects of your children's lives.

It's also likely that you will tend to measure their progress against the progress of your friends' children, and as long as you don't become too competitive about it, this will give you a guide in tracing their development.

Even at a very young age you want your children to lead a very full life and gain pleasure and satisfaction from what they are doing. So you will give them every opportunity to pursue interests and hobbies—anything from Brownies and Cubs to ballet, horse-riding, swimming clubs, adventure playgrounds, etc.

You also want them to have plenty of fun and enjoyment, to be able to mix well and share things with other children, so you will encourage them to be out-going and sociable. You are ambitious for your children and you have an ideal image of them as capable and accomplished people, perhaps with special talents and exceptional abilities. You look for excellence in them, but you are also realistic and can accept them and love them for what they are. The most important thing is for them to be themselves.

You allow your children to join in adult life so they can appreciate you and perhaps understand you as a person as well as a mother or father. You want a real relationship with them and you give them a great deal of attention and a lot of love and affection without sentimentality.

You have faith in your children as people, and if they become difficult, rebellious teenagers at any stage, you will probably cope extremely well. Although it may be an uncomfortable and sometimes worrying experience, you appreciate the fact that they are trying to 'find themselves' and you realize it is a necessary part of their growing up. So you are not likely to fall out with your teenagers—you are more likely to help them through emotional difficulties and to be sympathetic and understanding.

CONCLUSION THREE

You are a protective and indulgent parent. You identify very closely with your children and you give them warmth, security and unconditional love.

Your maternal/paternal instinct is extremely powerful, and you obtain a deep sense of joy and satisfaction in the process of bringing up children; they are part of you and you are more than prepared to devote yourself to them, to make sacrifices for them if necessary and to give them your full, undivided love and attention. You enjoy providing for them and making them happy.

You are sentimental about the mystique of childhood, and you probably enjoy reading fairy stories to them and watching their delight in Punch and Judy or Santa Claus. There will often be tears of joy in your eyes as you see their intense, childish happiness.

You are likely to be physically demonstrative, and your children will receive a lot of hugging and kissing and verbal endearment. They will feel truly loved.

You are fiercely loyal to them, you will defend your children right or wrong, and you will react very strongly to any outside criticism of them.

Your enjoyment of them may sometimes be marred by your tendency to worry about them. You are likely to get into a very anxious state if young children stray out of your sight or if school children are a bit late home. You will anticipate dangers and tend to imagine the worst. You will do everything in your power to avoid any possibility of danger.

A lot is said these days about the 'mistake' of over-protecting children, but it's better to over-protect than not to protect enough. If it is in your nature to be protective it will be almost impossible for you to stop caring so much, to stop being anxious about your fears. Other people may sometimes accuse you of being too 'fussy', but you rely on your strong instincts, and it would certainly be a mistake for you to go against your own deep intuitive feelings. You are a natural parent and you know what you are doing; you know what you feel is right.

As the children get older they may complain that you nag and fuss over them too much, that you don't allow them the same freedom of movement their friends enjoy, but they know they are truly loved and cared for, and that is far more important.

In any case it's very likely that as the children grow up you will gradually realize that they are becoming more and more sensible and able to look after themselves; and you will then gradually be able to extend their physical freedom and allow them to be more independent.

If your children become rebellious teenagers it is likely to be a difficult and perhaps nerve-wracking time for you. You will find it very hard to 'let go' of them. Your instinct will be to restrict their freedom for their own safety, but as you also want them to be popular with their own age group, to be happy and fulfilled, there will be a painful conflict between the desire to let them enjoy themselves, and the need to shield them against possible harm.

Even if there are temporary hostilities at this time, your children will know basically that you have been a good parent. The early experience of parental love will enable them to form good, loving relationships of their own.

Although you are obviously ambitious for your children, your feelings for them remain constant and unchanged whether they pass an examination or fail it, whether they behave well or badly. They have the security of knowing that you will always love them and that they can always turn to you for help and support, or simply for pleasure, affection and friendship.

CONCLUSION FOUR

You have an instinctive love for children and an instinctive understanding of them. In many ways you are as much a friend to them as a parent figure. Romping and playing with them is an important part of your communication with them.

You will join in their fun and laughter, you will enter fully into the spirit of the occasion on a picnic or family outing, and you will probably enjoy make-believe games with them. You treasure childhood as a very special time, embued with a sense of awe and magic. You want to share in your children's feelings and fantasies, to experience life *with* them. You value the qualities of childhood—the sense of wonder and imagination, the uninhibited behaviour, the intensity of feeling, the honesty and enthusiasm of children.

You are able to share all these things with them. You not only share their joys, but you also share their moments of misery and insecurity, their tears and tantrums. So you are likely to have a very close emotional relationship with your children. Sometimes you may be too emotionally involved to discipline them as much as you feel you ought to, for freedom of expression is something you encourage. Not only are the children free to express themselves, but you are too, so you will all exist on a highly emotional level. There will be times of chaos and emotional upheaval and times of wonderful love and laughter.

Rather than setting yourself up on a parental pedestal, you show the children that you are human, that just like them you can sometimes be in a bad mood, you can sometimes be extravagant in your behaviour and extreme in your emotions. The close friendship you have built up with your children enables them to accept and appreciate this. And if you are sometimes a bit lax in the practical details of their upbringing you more than make up for it by your spontaneous love and affection for them, by the creative atmosphere you engender and the deeply emotional bond which exists between you.

In a sense you put yourself at the children's level and grow up with them, adjusting yourself to their personalities as they develop and experiencing each stage with them. At times you almost feel you learn as much from them as they learn from you. You find out a great deal about yourself through the children, they add a new dimension to your personality, and they can also re-create and even improve your own childhood. Child-raising for you is a creative experience. You get to know your children very well indeed and there is never likely to be very much of a 'generation gap' between you. They won't be afraid to come to you with their problems and they won't be ashamed of admitting their deepest, innermost feelings to you.

When your children are teenagers you may be tempted to give them more freedom than is perhaps good for them, because you don't want to antagonize them and lose your good relationship with them, even temporarily. You will certainly sympathize with their desires and understand their problems, and assuming that no great traumas occur at this time, it is likely that you and the children can pass through their adolescent stage remaining the best of friends.

Put yourself in the place of the stick person in these cartoons, and try to gauge which of the alternatives would be nearest to your own reaction to each situation. Take time to think about each situation if necessary and answer as honestly as possible. Try to think how you really *would* respond, and not how you'd *like to* or think you *ought* to respond. Think of similar situations you've been in, and how you reacted then.

1.

(c) '*I* see! Well, if he's decided to be like that I'll get my business with him over quickly, but I'll make certain he attends to me properly anyway.'

(b) 'He's a bit brusque, isn't he? Must've had a bad day, I'll try to humour him.'

(d) 'How *dare* he treat me like that! I'll tell him what I think of him!'

(a) 'Oh Lord, I'm wasting his time. He's going to think I'm awfully stupid!'

2.

(d) Out loud: 'Good. Fine. But next time I think it would be even more effective if we etc., etc. . . .' Thinks: 'Huh! I'm the blue-eyed boy/girl now am I? So now's the time to strike!'

(b) Out loud: 'Oh, it's all right, I enjoyed it. It was nothing really.' Thinks: 'Fantastic! That's terrific! What a relief he liked it!'

(a) Smile of thanks. Thinks: 'So he damn well *should* be pleased—I worked hard enough over it!'

(c) Out loud: 'I'm glad you liked the results. You know I'm always interested in tackling this kind of project.' Thinks: 'Well, he's not such a bad old scoundrel really!'

(a) Make the gesture (rather hesitantly) of agreeing and being interested, but know you won't ever turn up at the hall.

(d) Tell him as politely as possible that you're extremely busy and don't have much spare time.

(c) Ask for details of what is involved, and say you'll come along when you have the opportunity. Determine to go, but probably not within the next week.

(b) Agree cheerfully and make a definite promise to go one day within the same week. In reality you are not as enthusiastic as you seem, but you're not against the idea either.

4.

(c) Refuse to be panicked. Be firm with her, explain why you're late and suggest she looks in her book to see whether the dentist might be able to fit you in. Give up only when you have exhausted all the possibilities.

(d) Become rather angry, argue with her and *insist* on being seen. If you still get nowhere with her, demand to talk to Mr Cheesman himself.

(a) Sigh, boil with frustration, acquiesce, leave hurriedly fuming to yourself.

(b) Apologize profusely, ask whether the dentist couldn't *please* find a space to see you. If she still refuses give in with a good grace—after all, it *was* your fault for being late.

(d) Indignantly: 'People don't want to buy stuff from shopkeepers who are so rude, either! If I'm going to buy something I've got a perfect right to look at it first. In fact, I won't bother!' Storm out.

(b) Surprised expression, light tone: 'Well really, sorry—I haven't got leprosy, you know!' Or some such quip.

(c) Disapproving expression, rather loud, reasoning tone: 'Well, I assure you I haven't done any harm.' Buy what you want with just a slightly sarcastic 'thank you' before you go.

(a) Take your hand away from the fruit, ignore the comment, buy what you want, stiffly, and go.

6.

(b) Feel really rather honoured to talk to the wonderful Norman and Jennifer, praise them and let them know you're impressed.

(d) Resent them immediately, refuse to be impressed, tell them about *your* achievements in the course of the conversation, perhaps exaggerating your own accomplishments a bit.

(a) Dislike the gushing hostess and resent the 'wonderful' couple yet feel a bit in awe of them. Wonder what on earth you're going to say to them and determine to escape from them as rapidly as possible.

(c) Feel rather amused by the gushing hostess. Question the 'wonderful couple' about their lives, being interested but not over-impressed.

7.

(a) Feel rather alarmed and a bit panic-struck. You don't really want to get involved, but you can't really refuse when someone throws themselves on your mercy like that.

(d) You feel a bit suspicious and wonder what he's up to. Why has he come to *you*? Hasn't he got friends or relatives he could go to? Ask what it's all about, but make no promises.

(b) Feel sorry for him, he is obviously desperate. Promise to help him straight away, even before you know what the problem is—there must be *something* you can do.

(c) Feel concerned for him and ask for details. Tell him you are sure you can advise him and suggest some course of action even if you are unable to help personally.

8.

(b) Feel shaken. Thank her for telling you, confide in her as an ally, ask her advice about what to do, etc.

(d) Dismiss her as a trouble-maker. Accuse her of malicious gossip and tell her you don't want to hear any more.

(c) Give her the benefit of the doubt, try to keep calm, question her to find out if she's telling the truth, and what is behind it all.

(a) Feel upset and confused. You're glad she told you so that you now know where you are with the others, yet at the same time you resent her for telling you. You are too choked-up to say very much to her at all.

9.

(c) 'I thought the arrangements were perfectly good as they were. What's the point of meeting at Ted and Sara's instead?'

(a) Shrug: 'Oh all right, if you prefer . . .' Silent offence— so why don't they want to come to *my* place?

(d) 'Well thanks for trying to change everything behind my back! It's too bad, I've organized everything now and I don't see any reason for changing the plan. You'll just have to come to me!'

(b) 'Yes, that's fine, if Ted and Sara's is more convenient for everyone. Good!'

10.

(b) Feel very stunned, hurt and embarrassed by the situation. Have you done something to offend them? Could they have just forgotten to mention it to you?

(a) Feel extremely insulted—that's a real slap in the face. Convince yourself you couldn't care less—you don't want to go to their rotten party anyway!

(c) Feel taken aback and puzzled. It's a bit odd to say the least. Feel sure they haven't excluded you deliberately; perhaps you'll phone up or call round to find out the answer to the mystery.

(d) Feel very scornful of them. Well, would you believe it —you always suspected that Bob/Melanie was jealous of you, and now you know for sure. Well, they're not getting away with it. Either you'll call round and make a scene about it or you'll just turn up at the party unannounced and see their reaction! Huh!

(a) You'd listen with apparent sympathy, but be secretly pleased she's upset because you feel she deserves to suffer for what she did.

(d) You'd tend to sit in judgement and show your disapproval openly, criticizing the way she handled the situation.

(b) You'd genuinely commiserate with her and try to comfort her and reassure her it wasn't her fault.

(c) You'd go through the details of the situation giving her your own interpretation of the events. You'd point out where she was to blame, and advise her what to do about it.

12.

(d) Get angry: 'Jack Smith—you clumsy idiot! ! ! *—! What did you do that for, you fool!'

(c) Accept Jack's apology, but warn; 'Just look where you're going next time!'

(a) Get huffed; sigh, mutter, mumble, make a display of rubbing your leg, elbow; respond to his apology with an irritable or sarcastic 'Oh, it's all right. Don't worry!'

(b) Make a joke of it: 'It's OK Jack, no permanent injury done I'm sure—you only half-killed me, that's all!'

(c) '*Do* stop making such a fuss about it—you're blowing it up out of all proportion. There's no harm done. I was perfectly justified, and I did it because etc., etc. . . .'

(b) 'I'm sorry, it was my fault, I didn't realize it was as bad as that, Oh heavens I feel terrible. I'm sorry, I'm really sorry . . .'

(d) 'Why should *I* apologise? *I* haven't done anything, and I've just about had enough of you and your complaints about me! If you don't like it you can—! *You're* the one who should be apologising!'

(a) 'Well I'm *sorry*! I didn't *mean* it. *Sorry*! I *apologise*!' Sink into silent sulk.

14.

(d) You take a dim view of it and will certainly tell the children's mother you cannot have them dumped on you like this.

(c) You don't mind too much. It means you can ask the children's parents a favour some time, but you will tell the mother to give you advance warning next time.

(a) You feel put-upon, but you'll probably pretend you don't mind the imposition when the children's mother comes to collect them.

(b) You're pleased to help out—it's so nice to have friendly neighbours.

15.

(a) Feel jealous and hurt: 'He/she's all right, I suppose.'
Drop the painful topic, but determine not to invite
Jeremy/Susan round again if you can avoid it.

(d) Feel personally insulted more than sexually jealous:
'Jeremy/Susan? What's so special about *him/her*?'
Think of as many down-grading remarks as you can.

(b) 'Well, yes, he/she *is* rather unusual really . . .' Try to
quell your feelings of jealousy; after all it's only
natural that your partner should fancy someone else
occasionally.

(c) Feel amused and just slightly wary rather than jealous: 'Oh, I see—you fancy Jeremy/Susan do you?
I'll have to watch out then!'

16.

(b) 'Yes, of course you can.'

(d) 'No, I want it myself.'

(c) 'You can if you promise to look after it. What do you want it for?'

(a) 'Well, er—Well yes I *suppose* you can if you really want to.'

17.

(d) 'Well, you know how busy I am—you shouldn't ask me to do these things for you in the first place. Go and collect your *own* clothes from the cleaners yourself next time!'

(b) 'I'm sorry, love/darling. How *could* I have forgotten?
I *am* sorry. I promise I'll remember tomorrow—I
really will make a special point of it.'

(a) 'Oh lord! I forgot! I'm sorry, but I haven't been feeling too well today/I had a lot on my mind. Well, I
said I was *sorry*!'

(c) 'Sorry, I forgot. Look, love/darling, I know I prom-
ised to do it for you, but could you please go to the
cleaners yourself tomorrow—I'm going to be far too
busy.'

18.

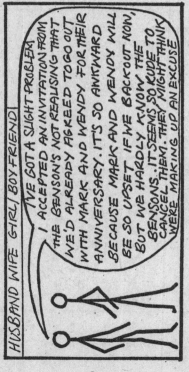

(b) 'Yes, I see what you mean. What are we going to do? Perhaps we ought to cancel Mark and Wendy instead . . . No, we can't very well do that. We'll just have to cancel the Bensons, I'm *sure* they'll understand if you explain to them, etc. . . .'

(c) 'What's the problem? Why should they think we're just making an excuse? Really there's no choice anyway, we can't let Mark and Wendy down on their anniversary. I'll ring the Bensons now and sort it out.'

(a) 'Oh God! Well, *I* don't know! It's nothing to do with me, you do what you think is best.'

(d) 'What a stupid muddle to get yourself into! Why can't you just *try* to be a bit more efficient? This is ridiculous.' You're the one who got us into this mess, it's up to you to get us out of it again!'

Turn to the SCORING PAGE.

SCORING PAGE

The Quiz divides into three sections, as laid out below: questions 1–6 make up SECTION ONE, questions 7–12 make up SECTION TWO, and questions 13–18 make up SECTION THREE.

Go through the completed quiz and mark which letter (a) (b) (c) or (d) you have scored for each question in the boxes below. Mark in your highest score at the end of each section. It may work out that you have scored equally highly for two categories, in which case enter both letters at the end of each section, and read the conclusions for both. For instance, the end of SECTION ONE may look like this—

Mostly $\boxed{a}$ or $\boxed{\diagup}$ and $\boxed{\diagup}$

Or it may look like this—

Mostly $\boxed{a}$ or $\boxed{d}$ and $\boxed{\diagup}$

Section One
Question Number   (*a*)   (*b*)   (*c*) *or* (*d*)

1 —
2 —
3 —
4 —
5 —
6 —

Mostly — ☐ or ☐ and ☐

Section Two

7 —
8 —
9 —
10 —
11 —
12 —

Mostly — ☐ or ☐ and ☐

164

13 —
14 —
15 —
16 —
17 —
18 —
Mostly — ☐ or ☐ and ☐

Now count up your scores for the whole Quiz, including all three sections, and make a note of your highest and second-highest scored categories:

Mostly — ☐
Second-highest score — ☐

Read conclusions for SECTIONS ONE, TWO and THREE, and then turn to the GENERAL SUMMING UP.

SECTION ONE—YOUR BEHAVIOUR WITH 'SUPERIORS'
Section One gives an indication of how you deal with people and social situations when you are at a disadvantage; how you cope with people who are in some way 'superior' to you: people in authority, people on a more elevated level of society, people who have some sort of power over you during a particular time.

Mostly (a)
Your behaviour is submissive to those in authority, yet it is obvious from your manner and your general demeanour that you feel angry and hostile towards them. You tend to be over-sensitive about your personal and social status, so that although you fear your 'superiors' you also resent them bitterly for making you feel 'inferior'.

Rather than having the courage to challenge them directly, you will be self-effacing but subversively difficult, retreating from them when possible, and only co-operating with them reluctantly.

In a working situation it is likely that you often resent taking orders and that you feel antagonistic to those in charge. You may feel you are being made to submit to situations which are beneath your dignity and your pride is constantly in danger of being wounded. You cannot accept a role as an underling, but you find it difficult to do anything about it.

Lack of confidence sometimes has a rather paralyzing effect, but it would be worth trying to either accept situations with a better grace, without taking them so personally, or else try to assert yourself more positively.

A lot of tension and bad feeling builds up because you tend to think that people are 'against' you; your own behaviour is likely to become more sullen as the resentment increases.

You tend to fear failure, and to fear being made to look foolish and this may prevent you from speaking out when you feel wronged and unappreciated.

The 'superior' people who come into contact with you often have difficulty in understanding your reaction to them. Many of them won't even be aware that you see them as being 'superior' at all, and they will be puzzled by your hostility. They are likely to interpret your manner as coldness and aloofness. In a job your attitude can work against you because people naturally prefer to give promotions and increased responsibility to those who are friendly and cheerful. You may sometimes get the reputation of being awkward and unsympathetic.

Try to build up your self-confidence gradually by asserting yourself more, speaking your mind and even being openly rebellious sometimes. Then at least people will know where they are with you; and people in authority usually respect you more if you challenge them when you feel you have a genuine grievance.

Mostly (b)

You tend to be submissive to people in authority, and you accept their power over you without resentment. You are inclined to be very influenced by the positions people hold, so that you see the boss as a boss rather than a person, and a doctor as a doctor and only secondarily a man or woman.

Of course this attitude makes it more difficult for them to treat you as an equal. They will see you as friendly and co-operative, always willing to help and to comply.

At work those in charge are likely to feel warm towards you and be grateful to you, as someone they can rely on and trust and as someone who always tries to carry out their work with a cheerful and pleasant manner and attitude. If other people are difficult and problematical, they know they will not have to worry about you.

But because they know you are easy-going and won't make a fuss, it's possible that they are sometimes tempted to give you an unfair burden of work, without giving you your rightful recognition and reward.

You have a genuinely helpful nature, but your compliance may also partly stem from a fear of falling out of grace with your 'superiors'. You respect and admire people you see as your 'superiors', you are very anxious to please them and to make a good impression on them. So you will avoid trouble and conflict with them, fearing their anger or disapproval and making sure you never have to incur it. Even when you know someone in authority has been less than kind to you, you tend to make excuses for them rather than facing up to them and challenging them.

You have probably learnt that you can often get your own way by being charming; and by making so much effort to be good and co-operative that people eventually feel they cannot refuse your requests.

When situations run smoothly and people in authority treat you well, you are likely to have very good relationships with them, and they will appreciate your charm and willingness to oblige. However, when people in authority treat you badly a little bit of aggression on your part would be a good thing. You treat other people with consideration so you must make sure they treat *you* with the same care and fairness. The sad fact is that very often if people think you'll accept second best, they'll try to get away with it.

Mostly (c)

You are dominant and able to assert yourself with people in authority, yet you can remain friendly and unresentful of their power. You are not afraid of them, nor do you imbue them with any special qualities or virtues simply because of their 'superior' status. You respect people for what they *are* rather than for the positions they hold. You do not feel they are better than you simply because they may hold a higher social or work position.

This means that your career prospects should be very good. You can take sensible orders willingly, you can co-operate with authority figures in a friendly spirit, without feeling threatened or diminished as a person.

Your attitude towards 'superiors' makes it easy for them to treat you as an equal. They are likely to recognize your self-confidence and to respect your opinions. They will listen to you seriously and trust your judgements because they know there is no fear and no bitterness in your feelings towards them.

You give an impression of competence, maturity and strength of character. Your natural inclination is to be peaceful and friendly, to be helpful and obliging and to maintain good, co-operative relationships. But when someone treats you badly—no matter how elevated their position—you will stand up for yourself. You judge people on human terms and you deal with them on human terms.

People in authority over you will soon realize that they cannot use their position of power to overrule you or coerce you in any way. You give others fair treatment, and you expect fair treatment in return. You will make sure that your demands are met.

You are able to behave freely and naturally in the company of 'superiors', because you are neither desperate for their approval, nor fearful of their disapproval. They do not worry you, for you know you can always cope with trouble from them if it crops up. As a rule the concept of 'superior' and 'inferior' doesn't concern you at all.

Mostly (d)
You can obviously look after yourself and cope with people in authority, refusing to be impressed by them and determined to prove that you're as good or better than they are.

You enjoy contests with them and feel it is rather impressive to make a display of aggression towards them, and to take a 'bolshy' attitude. You take every opportunity to assert yourself, and although others may resent you and complain about you, they often have a sneaking admiration for your courage in facing up to opposition, even courting it sometimes.

You are very conscious of status and position and you bitterly resent people who have any kind of power over you. Because you cannot bear to accept an 'inferior' role you often feel extremely hostile towards someone because of their 'superior' position rather than their human qualities as a person. This means that in any situation where you think your dignity might be at risk, you are likely to overreact and become antagonistic, so your understanding of the situation is bound to be limited.

Sometimes your aggression will work for you—you certainly get yourself noticed, and you've probably learnt by experience that if you make a fuss and refuse to give up people often become worn down enough to give in to you.

In a job you will probably have difficulty in accepting other people's authority and in getting on with your 'superiors'. You may get the reputation for being difficult and a troublemaker, though in some competitive jobs your forceful, dominating manner may be a positive advantage as long as you don't upset your working companions too much.

You give the impression of being tough and aggressive, and others may also see you as being over-ambitious and rather an opportunist, exploiting situations to your advantage whenever you can. The more status and responsibility you are given, the less hostile you will become. If you are commanding and managing you will feel you have reached your rightful position in life and can drop some of your defences. If you feel neglected and overruled, you will put up a fight for supremacy.

In general you are trying too hard to prove yourself—a more relaxed, friendly attitude may get you where you want to go more quickly, and certainly more pleasantly.

SECTION TWO—YOUR BEHAVIOUR WITH EQUALS

Section Two gives an indication of how you deal with people you see as your equals—your friends and acquaintances—how you cope with social situations.

Mostly (a)

You tend to be rather suspicious and defensive in social situations, quick to imagine the' worst and to feel slighted. In friendships there is sometimes a feeling that you're on your guard and fearful of being hurt or betrayed.

Basically you need a lot of reassurance that people really do like you and accept you, and friends have to prove their good intentions towards you before you will give your friendship completely. You often seem to hold back, being rather secretive and difficult to get to know because you find it hard to open out to people emotionally.

Shyness is partly to blame for this, but although others recognize your reserve they may also notice an undercurrent of hostility sometimes. You may therefore give the false impression of being aloof, critical and disinterested, and your manner may make people wary of approaching you.

Tending to be consumed with your own feelings, you forget that other people are also shy and afraid of being snubbed and made to look silly. Rather than risking the indignity of being snubbed, they may avoid you or adopt a hostile manner themselves for self-protection. You are sensitive to their signs of hostility and defensiveness, so you respond in kind, and a chain-reaction is set up. Barriers between people build up in this way. People fear each other initially and unless they can make friendly gestures and break down the uncertainty, a hostile atmosphere will develop. That's why it's up to *you* to go at least half way in offering friendship and approval. People will begin to react to you differently if you treat them differently.

With friends and in social groups you probably give the

impression of being rather moody, unpredictable in your reactions and difficult to understand. This is because you don't always make your true feelings known; you tend to bottle up resentment without questioning people and giving them a chance to explain their actions and motives. People don't always know they've offended you unless you tell them, so while you are smouldering with unexpressed anger, *they* will be wondering why you are acting so strangely. A lot of the hostility and wariness will disappear if you can get your feelings out into the open.

You become nicer and more friendly towards people as your self-confidence grows and you become more relaxed. Ironically, close friends often value your friendship more if they've had a difficult start with you—if people have disliked you or been unsure of you in the past their feeling of liking is often made stronger for the struggle in overcoming hostilities.

In general it's likely that people see you as a 'deep' and sensitive person, a rather uncomfortable person at times, but a worthwhile challenge if they want to take you on!

Mostly (b)

You tend to be slightly shy and unsure of yourself in social situations, but it's obvious that you want to make friends, that you are genuinely interested in people and anxious to show them your approval and goodwill.

You are keen for people to like you and to find you charming, and you react emotionally to them if they treat you with warmth and affection. You value friendship highly. You set great store by making new friends, possibly seeing them partly as social conquests and therefore a living proof of the effects of your charm. Meeting people for the first time is the most difficult hurdle for you, as you tend to suffer from an initial lack of self-confidence with people. This may be partly due to the fact that you're *too* anxious to please them and too concerned about the impression you're making on them.

In social life generally you often tend to be submissive and rather over-generous in your emotions and attitudes; too willing, at times, to give someone the benefit of the doubt, to placate them and smooth out potential conflict if you see it coming. You will more than go out of your way to avoid hostility, and you find it very difficult to cope with antagonism. You will be tempted to give way immediately and to 'turn a blind eye' to the shabbiness of other people's behaviour rather than risking an unpleasant confrontation. Others may sometimes take advantage of you because of this; and may sometimes fail to consider your feelings and wishes enough.

You tend to be too afraid of losing the good will and affiliation of others, and it's worth realizing that people will *still* like you even if you challenge them and criticize them sometimes. They may even like and respect you more for asserting yourself.

However, you are a rewarding person to know—you give people the feeling that you are really listening to them, paying attention to them and responding to them emotionally. So you should be very popular and appreciated, especially by your close friends. People can relax with you and confide in you. You are supportive to your friends, giving them a sense of security because they know your feelings towards them are genuine and constant.

In general you give the impression of being humanitarian, sincere and sympathetic.

Mostly (c)
Your relationships with equals are truly equal. You can approach people openly, with good will and friendship. Because you are not afraid of censure or disapproval, you can express yourself and reveal your personality to others without either artifice or an attempt to hide your feelings. You are more concerned about communicating with people than about making a good impression on them.

Your judgements and emotions remain clear and unconfused because you can be objective about people and situations; you seek the truth about your relationships rather than convincing yourself that what you want to believe is true.

You are dominant yet friendly in your dealings with friends and acquaintances; you generally feel that you are in command of relationships, that you have an equal say in things and an equal chance of taking charge and calling the tune. You are prepared to be friendly and easy-going until you are challenged or threatened, and then you can defend yourself with the conviction that you're right to do so. So you can cope with aggression when it arises.

You have the self-confidence to be true to yourself in your relationships, and you can command respect without asking for it.

Your motives are direct and genuine and this makes it easy for others to respond to you in the same spirit of trust and friendship. You are at ease and self-confident in social situations. You seem to have an air of authority which comes quite naturally to you, so you may often find yourself falling into a position of being a leader in the group. But people can accept your authority without resentment because they know you are not using them to boost your own ego or prove your own power.

You are helpful and sympathetic with a basic respect for other people and an in-built moral code which allows you to treat them with justice and consideration, but never to pander to them and ingratiate yourself.

In general you give the impression of being self-confident and approachable, a strong, forceful personality who is at the same time kind and willing to accept others as equals.

Mostly (d)
You are obviously rather aggressive and dominating in social situations and you make no secret of the fact that you want to be the leader, the one everyone has to listen to.

You are socially competitive and sometimes enjoyment of the occasion and of communication with others take second place to your desire to prove yourself. So your social life tends to have an undercurrent of hostility, and it's likely that you often get into arguments, making enemies as fast as you make friends.

You are quick to respond aggressively at the first sign of a challenge or slight, consciously guarding your personal status and trying to win power and prestige. If you don't think someone is worth fighting against, in other words if you have labelled them as 'inferior', you are likely to dismiss them rather contemptuously.

Popularity as such is less important to you than recognition as a dominant personality. You give the impression of extreme self-confidence, yet your anxiety constantly to prove how good you are shows that it requires tremendous effort for you to keep up the image of yourself you wish to perpetuate.

Some people will see you as a challenge and admire your social courage, others will dislike you but this won't generally worry you a lot—the worst thing is to be ignored or treated with indifference.

Friends are usually rivals too, and you will try to out-do them and out-talk them, sometimes with hostility and sometimes in a jocular, friendly manner.

Sometimes you can hurt people, being so preoccupied with your own image and your own motives that you fail to understand the effect you're having on them. At other times, perhaps to prove that you're not all bad, you can make gestures of extreme kindness and generosity, though this of course will add to your image as a 'larger than life' person.

You want to manipulate people through the force of your personality and you often have a stimulating, enlivening effect on a social group. People often realize that you're acting or at least exaggerating and overreacting, and they will find you entertaining and interesting.

In general you give the impression of being a dynamic, difficult person, lively, assertive, obstinate and fearless, though some may recognize the vulnerable side of your character.

SECTION THREE—YOUR BEHAVIOUR IN CLOSE RELATIONSHIPS

Section Three gives an indication of how you cope with close relationships and family relationships—how your behaviour with them is likely to affect the way they respond to you.

Mostly (a)
In close relationships you often tend to be rather secretive, to back out and evade issues you don't want to face. People around you may get the feeling that you are not involved or committed enough. You may give them the impression that they have failed you in some way, but as you don't always express your feelings, they will find it hard to understand what you want from them.

If they are determined to make you participate more, they may resort to nagging and criticism, or they may be discouraged and retreat from you.

You tend to be easily irritated and over-sensitive to subtle hints of disapproval and criticism, and this can lead to prolonged hostility unless you come out into the open more and try to solve emotional conflicts. You are more likely to take out your anger on small quarrels than to get to grips with the real issues. The trouble is that you don't always give other people the chance to get close to you. Problems are often difficult to overcome because your pride won't allow you to recognize failure in yourself and admit you are wrong sometimes. You may punish others by withdrawing your affection from them and making them feel insecure.

You can be loving and emotionally-expressive when your life is running smoothly and when other people show their regard and affection for you. But you do need encouragement. You can respond to the love and friendship of those close to you, but you are not so good at initiating the warmth and intimacy; perhaps because you are embarrassed by it; perhaps because you fear being rebuffed; perhaps because you need to *be* loved more than you need to love.

In sexual relationships you can be demonstrative and passionate when you are sure of the other person's love. The more you are made to feel loved, appreciated and desired, the more you are enabled to express your deepest feelings. You are likely to be jealous and possessive, and love can turn to hatred if you feel the other person has let you down or betrayed you. You won't forgive or forget. If the other person can cope with your moods and love you despite them, you should have a happy and intense relationship. Being loved and desired sexually is an extremely powerful need, not only for the pleasure of the experience, but also as a means of increasing your self-esteem, and as a means of expressing emotion which would not otherwise find an outlet.

Mostly (b)

You are sympathetic and easy-going in your close relationships. Rather than contempt, familiarity breeds loyalty and affection, a friendly interest in the preoccupations of people around you, and a genuine concern for their happiness and welfare.

You make people feel appreciated and needed. They know you are 'on their side', that you care about them and feel closely involved in their lives. You make it obvious that you are well-disposed towards them, so they are likely to respond to you in the same generous and pleasant manner, and your relationships should be free from petty tensions and hostilities and from the corroding effects of 'scoring points' against each other.

When a relationship runs into trouble you are likely to

blame yourself rather than blaming the other person. You are extremely generous in making allowances for the other person's behaviour. Your reaction may often be to subjugate your own wishes and to deny your own hurt feelings for the sake of peace and harmony.

You can give way to the demands of those around you gracefully, without rancour or resentment, although you are probably aware that it would sometimes be in your best interests to stick up for yourself more. But as long as your warmth and kind-heartedness are not abused you are able to create a loving and caring atmosphere, a sense of unity with those around you.

In sexual relationships you are tender and responsive. Although you naturally receive pleasure, your main concern is to give pleasure and happiness to the other person. It is important to you to be loved, but still more important to express your loving feelings. Even during times when the other person doesn't respond to you as you would wish, you remain unshaken in your devotion to your partner. Once you are deeply in love you won't give up easily—it takes a great deal to destroy your love.

Although the other person is the more dominating and active partner, your strength is your constancy, and your faith in the power of love.

Sometimes, however, you fail to have enough self-confidence, and because of this you may be *too* grateful for the love and attention of your partner, acquiescing too much, and not demanding enough. Appreciate your own real worth more if you want the relationship to be on more equal terms. However, you are able to obtain great happiness and satisfaction from a sexual union, making full use of your emotional sensitivity and your passionately tender feelings.

Mostly (c)
You convey a sense of friendship and equality in your close relationships. You can be mature, authoritarian and ob-

jective, yet you give those around you the feeling that you are emotionally involved with them, that you wish to share their interests and concerns, that you are committed to them.

Your instinct is to take control of situations, but if you dominate people you do so unobtrusively, advising them rather than telling them what to do; reasoning rather than arguing, influencing rather than persuading, directing rather than bullying. You are helpful and co-operative, and even when you set yourself up as the 'boss' you still make it known to people that their feelings and opinions count for something, so that you can very often get your own way without undermining their self-confidence.

Those around you are likely to respond to your kind but assertive behaviour by respecting you and returning your love and appreciation. You make others feel secure. They know they can trust your emotional integrity; they know your feelings are sincere; they know where they are with you because you can express your disapproval as well as your approval, your anger as well as your love. Above all, you are fair in your treatment of those close to you. You will forestall a great deal of conflict and petty tension and hostility by being willing to accept blame sometimes, by being open and expressive enough to avoid misunderstandings, and by dealing with conflicts promptly and without undue antagonism.

You manage to achieve a good balance between unselfish concern for others and asserting your own wishes and demands within relationships.

Your sexual relationships are likely to be characterized by the same balance of pleasing the other person and being pleased yourself. You are able to share your emotions and you are likely to be uninhibited about expressing your love, both physically and verbally. Your attitude to sex is that it is an activity of equals, so you can be passionate but understanding, loving but not prone to unreasonable jealousy. It's likely that you feel secure about your own sexuality, so that you won't be obsessed with sex for its own sake, and you won't use it for ulterior motives such as a means of gaining power over the other person, or a means of proving your desirability and boosting your self-esteem.

Mostly (d)

Your close relationships tend to be difficult and stormy, and your feelings towards those around you are often antagonistic. Up to a point, familiarity can often lead to contempt, and you sometimes fail to consider the feelings of others, using them to off-load your own anger or frustration. So you will be quick to pick fights with them, and to blame them when conflicts crop up. You want your own way; you want to be the dominant person in the family or group and you react aggressively if you think anyone might try to usurp your position of power.

Perhaps you are not sufficiently aware of the effect you are likely to have on those who are close to you. Perhaps they try to humour you. Perhaps they keep things from you when they think your knowledge of an event or situation would lead to an angry outburst and a generally unpleasant atmosphere. Perhaps they let you have your own way for the sake of peace—it just depends how much they fear your wrath, and how far they are prepared to be dominated by you.

Sometimes it seems you're almost *looking* for things to get heated and hostile about, so people around you are likely to feel tense and on edge. You tend to judge them harshly, and to resist their influence. In hostile situations you will be highly critical of others and unwilling to accept any responsibility for the bad feeling caused. In fact when you know you have behaved badly or unreasonably your guilt only seems to cause greater anger.

As you tend to go to extremes it's very likely that you can be extra loving, charming and attentive when you're pleased with your family or close relationships. If they can cope with your aggression and unpredictable behaviour, you should get away with it. Otherwise to improve harmony, either you will have to tone yourself down or *they* will have to adjust to your ways and accept you as you are.

In sexual relationships you again feel the need to be the dominant personality, the 'best' one of the couple. Even though you are capable of passionate love, both in sex and in emotional expression, you tend not to be relaxed enough for pure enjoyment of the situation. Your sexual life is usually partly motivated by a desire to gain control of your partner, to have power over them, and also to increase your own self-esteem through the manifestation of your sexual power and attraction.

GENERAL SUMMING UP

Look back to the Scoring Page of this Quiz to find your two top-scoring categories in the three sections overall.

Mostly (a) *and* (b) would indicate that in dealing with people in general your behaviour tends to be non-assertive, that in many situations you avoid drawing attention to yourself, often submitting to the demands of others, rather than making demands yourself.

Mostly (c) *and* (d) would indicate a general tendency to be assertive and dominating, to challenge people and take control of situations.

Mostly (b) *and* (c) would indicate that the most noticeable aspect of your behaviour is your general feeling of friendship and goodwill towards people. Whether you are being submissive or dominant your approach is affiliative —you put over the message that you basically like people.

Mostly (a) *and* (d) would indicate that the most noticeable aspect of your behaviour is a certain guardedness or hostility, as though part of you is standing back, judging and speculating rather than taking encounters with people on face value. Whether you are being submissive or dominant, you convey the message that you're not going automatically to accept the other person, that you cannot be 'won-over' so easily.

Mostly (*a*) *and* (*c*) would indicate that your behaviour with people changes quite a lot depending on your own mood and on the particular situation. As a rule your submissive behaviour is accompanied by feelings of threat and hostility, while your assertive behaviour is accompanied by friendly feelings. Seen the other way round, this means that when you're feeling hostile your instinct is to withdraw rather than to express your anger openly. When you're feeling friendly and self-confident your instinct is to assert yourself.

Mostly (*b*) *and* (*d*) would indicate that your behaviour with people changes quite a lot depending on your own mood and on the particular situation. As a rule your submissive behaviour is accompanied by friendly feelings, and your dominant, assertive behaviour is accompanied by hostile feelings. Seen the other way round this means that when your feelings are friendly your instinct is to be easy-going and compliant. When your feelings are hostile your instinct is to assert yourself and express your anger.

Now look back again at the Scoring Page to find out how consistent your scores are, taking the three sections of the quiz separately.

Did you land in the same category in all three sections (three (a)'s, or three (b)'s, etc.)?

Did you land in two of the same category and an odd one (two (d)'s and one (b), for example)?

Did you land in different categories at the end of each of the three sections (one (a), one (c) and one (d) for instance)?

The point is that most people play many social roles, and often behave quite differently in each of them, using different social styles, putting across different social images of themselves, and coping in different ways according to where they are and who they are with.

One person, for instance, may be relaxed, easy-going and submissive at home, hostile and dominant at work, assertive and friendly with friends and on social occasions.

Someone else may be dominating and hostile at home, yet shy, submissive and anxious to please at work. Yet a third person can be friendly and assertive at home, shy, submissive and hostile on social occasions, and hostile but dominant at work.

So there are many combinations, and by comparing your categories scored in each of the three sections you will get an idea of the areas in your life where you cope best and feel happiest and most relaxed, the areas where you feel most self-confident and assertive, the areas where you feel most stressed, uncomfortable or threatened. Perhaps you can find out which aspects of your life need changing or improving. Perhaps when you have located the areas of difficulty you can try to change your approach in these areas, to try to improve relationships and work out a better pattern of behaviour for coping with the situation.

For instance if you were (a) in Section One and (d) in Section Three the chances are that because you feel your position at work is ignominious and you feel helpless and undervalued, you are compensating for your sense of failure and frustration by taking out your anger and hostility on your family or close relationships. In this case it would obviously be a good thing for you to change your job or fight back and assert yourself more at work, so that you don't go back home with a backlog of anger to be released on the 'innocent victims'. If you increase your feeling of dominance and self-confidence at work, you will feel more relaxed and friendly at home.

If you were (b) in Section Two, for instance, and (c) in Section Three, you cope magnificently with close relationships, being self-confident, assertive, yet friendly and relaxed, so it might be worth asking yourself why you tend to be diffident in social situations. You can obviously express your feelings and your personality, and if you could make more of an immediate friendly impact outside your home and your close relationships, your social life would be enriched.

183

These are just two examples, but you can study your own scores and draw your own conclusions.

If your scores are consistent through the three sections your behaviour is consistent in most aspects of your life, you have a unified identity and you are particularly true to yourself, tending not to let your reactions be influenced by social pressures.

If your scores are different through the three sections you behave differently in different social situations, and you see a different image of yourself in contrasting roles— you are one person to your boss, another person to your friends, another person to your family, and so on. You express different aspects of your personality with different people. You tend to see your life split up into separate segments, to compartmentalize, and for this reason you may sometimes feel uncomfortable when the 'segments' are mixed up. You may avoid introducing one group of friends to another group, for instance, or you may feel ill at ease when a work-mate meets a member of your family, or when an old friend meets one of your newly acquired friends.

LOVE QUIZ

Tick the most appropriate answer to each question.

1. Which feelings do you mostly associate with falling in love?
   - (b) The depth of feeling, and the feeling of being enriched as a person.
   - (a) The emotional joy, which seems to put you on to another plane of existence.
   - (c) The pure thrill and feeling of well-being.

2. Is it most important to you that the person you love—
   - (e) should make a good impression on people?
   - (f) should have good religious or moral values?
   - (d) should have many interests in life?

3. Look at the picture below. Which explanation appeals to you most?

   - (c) It is their first experience of sexual love.
   - (a) It's about teenage dreams—an unconsummated, yearning kind of love.

(b) The boy and girl are very young, but it is a powerful mature, adult kind of love.

4. Which would be most important in your ideal partner?

    (f) Good-heartedness and sincerity.

    (d) Insight and understanding.

    (e) Self-confidence and a sociable nature.

5. Do you find this postcard—

VIEW FROM BRIGHTON PIER

    (a) Crude/insulting.

    (c) Funny.

    (b) Quaint/silly, but harmless.

6. If you were to imagine the perfect love affair for you, which setting or environment would you choose for it?

    (d) An arty or bohemian set of creative people who express themselves freely.

    (e) An affluent jet-set of glamorous people, luxurious living, etc.

    (f) An away-from-it-all setting—desert island, mountain village, sea-side cottage, etc.

7. Which colours would you imagine for the *décor* of the room?
   (b) Red/orange.
   (c) Yellow/brown.
   (a) Blue/purple.

8. If the picture above depicts a clandestine love affair, and both people are married/have steady relationships with other people, which explanation would you choose?
   (f) They are both unhappy with their regular partners but find loving care and emotional fulfilment with each other.
   (d) They were just friends with common interests and a mental rapport between them. They didn't mean to start an affair, but the relationship developed into love.
   (e) The affair just started for the fun, excitement and sexual attraction.

9. Which statement about the difficulties of love do you most agree with?
   (a) There nearly always seems to be an element of suffering in love, usually because one person loves the other more than they are loved in return.
   (c) Boredom with each other is the most difficult thing to prevent after a while in a love relationship.
   (b) Feelings become so strong and confused that love can easily turn to hatred.

10. Which of the following qualities would you look for most in a long-term partner?
   (e) Ambition and sophistication.
   (d) Intelligence and curiosity.
   (f) Compassion and constancy.

11. How would you sum up the general feeling and atmosphere of this picture?

   (c) A sense of evil joy and erotic pleasure.
   (b) A sense of profound meaning and involvement.
   (a) A sense of awsome mystery and spiritual wonder.

12. Which unhappy feeling do you suffer most in relationships (or which would you find hardest to bear)?

    (f) Emotional neglect—that tenderness is lacking, that people don't really care about you.

    (e) Lack of recognition—that people don't appreciate your qualities and accomplishments, that they think nothing of you and look down on you.

    (d) Mental and emotional isolation—that people don't respond to you, that you cannot find anyone to talk to who will understand you, that you can only communicate superficially and meaninglessly.

13. In this dramatic situation how do you imagine the cloaked figure would react?

    (b) Jealous rage—he feels like getting a dagger and killing the other man.

    (a) Utter despair and anguish—he feels like killing himself.

    (c) A demonic sense of mad revenge—he feels like playing some diabolical trick on them.

14. When the first flush of excitement and romance fades in a relationship, which of the following do you think it is most important to retain?
    (d) That you still find each other interesting as people.
    (f) That you still have a sense of loyalty and commitment to each other.
    (e) That you still respect and admire each other's aims in life.

15. Which of the following is nearest your own feelings about casual sex relationships without love?
    (c) They can be fun, exciting and harmless.
    (a) They are all wrong, morally and/or emotionally.
    (b) Basically they are just not satisfying or emotionally rewarding enough.

16.

If the picture illustrates a mythical story, which of
the following stories appeals to you most?

(f) They have both been blinded by a witch's spell
and are trying to lead each other across the
desert to safety.

(e) The man has some kind of power or spell over
the girl, and although she fears him she finds
herself compelled to fall in love with him.

(d) They have got to find the Fountain of the
Secret of Life. If they do not find it they are
doomed, but if they find it they can live happily
together for ever.

17. If you were to write a love poem, do you think the
general tone would most likely be—

(b) wild, desperate, dramatic?

(c) sensual, pornographic?

(a) sensitive, lingering, haunting?

18. Meeting someone of the opposite sex for the first time, which of the following would put you off most?
    (e) Badly groomed and dressed.
    (d) Boring conversation.
    (f) Casual, off-hand manner.
19. Which is most often most appealing to you in physical sex?
    (a) A sense of beauty and aestheticism.
    (c) A sense of humour and playfulness.
    (b) A sense of fervour, overpowering intensity.
20. and 21.

20. Apart from sexual motives, what is the attraction for the man to the gypsy girl?
    (d) He is intrigued, fascinated by the differences in their outlooks and life-styles.
    (e) He idolizes her—she is like his fantasy image of a gypsy girl transposed into reality.
    (f) He feels a strong emotional magnetism—she symbolizes all the good natural qualities he has lost through sophistication and 'progress'.

21. If the couple in the picture were the hero and heroine of a Hollywood film, do you see the basic theme as—
    (b) scandalous love—censure?
    (a) forbidden love—secrecy?
    (c) permissive love—freedom?

22. Do you find you are mostly attracted to—
    (e) people who are successful in the eyes of the world?
    (f) people who are friendly and warm?
    (d) people who are unusual or original in some way?

23. and 24.

23. In this picture do you think the woman is—
    (c) seducing and encouraging the man?
    (b) responding equally to him?
    (a) yielding to him?

24. In the picture do you think the man's feelings are concerned with—
    (f) sentiment and devotion to the woman?
    (d) soulfulness and spiritual affinity with the woman?
    (e) conquest and admiration for the woman?

Now see SCORING PAGE.

SCORING PAGE

The Love Quiz is a guide to the needs of your personality in relation to other people. It is also a barometer of the conditions of your love life.

It is part of human nature never to be quite satisfied enough with what we have. If a particular need is being fulfilled we tend to underestimate its importance, and if a need is unfulfilled the tendency is to overestimate its importance.

If you have a very secure relationship, for instance, you may begin to crave for more uncertainty and excitement; and if you have a very exciting relationship you may crave for more security.

Each category in the quiz represents a need and the object is to put each need into its order of importance for you.

The needs for which you have a low score or no score at all could indicate one of two things. Either the need is so satisfied that you take it for granted, or the need is not important to you. A highly scored need is one which is always important to you, or one which is unfulfilled at the moment.

With the aid of the table below, count how many points you have scored for (a) (b) (c) (d) (e) and (f), marking a zero beside categories where you have scored nothing. Then place them in order (1–6) from the highest to the lowest scored category.

Number of Points	*Order of Importance*
(a) — ☐	1. — ( )
(b) — ☐	2. — ( )
(c) — ☐	3. — ( )
(d) — ☐	4. — ( )
(e) — ☐	5. — ( )
(f) — ☐	6. — ( )

Now read CONCLUSIONS for ALL categories (a)–(f), noting their order of importance for you.

Need (a)—ROMANTIC LOVE
Placed ☐ in your personal scale of importance.

This need really has more to do with courtship than sex, although sexual desire enters into the need for romance. It is primarily a longing for mutual adoration and self-glorification. You want to be lifted out of the ordinary into a world of poetic beauty and ecstasy; to experience a wonderful feeling of heightened sensitivity, a feeling of magic and enchantment, of fate and destiny; to glorify the love relationship; to bring the realms of fantasy and imagination into living reality.

Romantic love has a fleeting, illusory quality and the craving for romance can mostly only be satisfied through films and novels, through day-dreams, though sometimes it can be satisfied through real relationships. Of course the illusiveness of romance makes it even more appealing, but basically everyone, to a degree, would like romantic dreams to come true. Even though the need may seldom be admitted everyone would like to be made to feel that they are the most wonderful, special and extraordinary person in the world.

Need (b)—EMOTIONAL AND SEXUAL PASSION
Placed ☐ in your personal scale of importance.

This is the need for deep, powerful feeling, for emotional extremes. It is the antithesis of indifference, of 'plodding on' in a relationship, of skating over the surface without heights or depths of feeling.

It is a craving for drama, even tragedy; for strong emotion to let you know that you are really 'living', that your relationship is full of meaning and intensity; that you are not just existing, not wasting any of the richness of human passion. You want to experience everything that it is possible for a human being to experience. You want to discover the force of grand emotions and to this end you long for a relationship which enables you to express and explore your own emotions, and which satisfies all your most powerful, primeval and unfathomable feelings.

Sexually you long for the same sense of grand passion and meaning. You want both you and your partner to be totally involved—with body, mind and soul totally concentrated on each other and on your experience together.

Passion, like romantic love, is another thing which tends to be swept away in the routine and mundanities of everyday life but everyone, at some time or another, wishes that relationships could be more expressive and demonstrative, more imbued with pungency and significance.

Need (c)—EROTIC LOVE
Placed ☐ in your personal scale of importance.

Love is not the most important element in this need, though love may also be present. It is the need to satisfy the sensual desires of the body; the need for sexual pleasure and abandonment; the longing to indulge your senses, to throw caution and restraint to the wind and to gratify your sexual whims and desires.

It is the basic need for pure physical enjoyment, for the expression of powerful but often guilt-ridden urges. For many people this need is the most difficult to come to terms with because of inhibitions and moral codes which prevent them from acting out their fantasies or make them feel bad if they do. It is often partially satisfied through pornography and imagination. It is often denied altogether, but everyone at least secretly craves for a sexual relationship which enables them to experience the heights of physical joy, and which satisfies their erotic dreams and desires.

Also associated with this need is the longing for fun, excitement and adventure.

Need (d)—MENTAL STIMULATION AND
              EMOTIONAL AFFINITY
              Placed ☐ in your personal scale of importance.

This is the need for a soul-mate, for a kindred spirit to whom you can express your feelings and ideas; someone who thinks and feels the same way as you do, who is in tune with your views and attitudes and who reacts emotionally to life much the same way as you do.

It is the need to be inspired and stimulated mutually; to add new dimensions to each other's lives, to aid and encourage each other to grow and expand, mentally, spiritually and emotionally.

There is a wish to be raised up to a higher level of thought and feeling through a relationship; to be endlessly curious, fascinated and intrigued; to achieve a special communication of esoteric understanding; to be able to express and develop philosophical and emotionally complicated ideas with someone who is as absorbed and interested as you are; someone who recognizes and sympathizes with your higher aims in life.

Most of the time relationships are carried out on a practical level of shared activities and shared 'down to earth' pleasures and preoccupations. But there are also times when everyone longs for deep emotional communication; for a heart-to-heart; for a chance to analyze themselves and the world with a fellow-traveller. Everyone sometimes longs to express the spiritual and metaphysical side of the personality—to be heard, to be understood, to be reassured that feelings and beliefs are endorsed and shared by someone else.

Need (e)—STATUS AND SELF-ESTEEM
              Placed ☐ in your personal scale of importance.

This is an exhibitionist instinct to show off, to stand out from the crowd, to gain attention and admiration from other people. It is the need to enhance your prestige and self-esteem through your relationships.

If this need is strong the qualities prized by the world are those you look for in your partner. Money, success, attractiveness, for instance are important as image-builders. You want to be able to admire and respect someone, to raise your own self-esteem through standing in their reflected glory, and identifying with their power, magnetism, success, etc.

The need also encompasses a longing to be admired and appreciated by a loving partner—the more adulation you receive the more your self-confidence grows and the more you are encouraged to develop and expand those appreciated qualities; the more you can delight in your accomplishments and ambitions. Achievements apart, there is also a need to be admired as a person, for your intrinsic personality, for the natural qualities you were born with—your looks, your gracefulness, your voice, and so on.

Few people get a chance to shine out from the herd, but genuine compliments, approval and applause from just one other person can fulfil the need for status and self-esteem.

Even if they don't like to admit it, everyone wants to be noticed, respected and praised. Everyone would like to feel that they are in some way superior to other people.

Need (f)—SECURITY, COMPANIONSHIP AND
         CONTENTMENT
         Placed ☐ in your personal scale of importance.

This is the need for genuine love and affection, for a close identity with someone else and for a sense of security in a relationship. It is the need for someone with all the true, old-fashioned virtues, for a relationship of peace and harmony, of trust and honesty; a relationship which is eternally good and reliable.

This is part of a basic need for safety and well-being.

You want to know where you are with someone. You want a real companion in life; someone you can be contented and at peace with; someone who is inseparable from you, whose fears, wishes, concerns, and hopes are your own in unshakable togetherness.

Liberated and permissive ideas about relationships have brought with them a lot of uncertainty and anxiety. However liberated people are, there is still a basic need for exclusive commitment; for the feeling that you never have to be lost or lonely, that whatever happens in your life you will always have someone to love and comfort you.

Everyone at some point longs for a relationship which is free from strife and turmoil, from jealousy and insecurity, from harshness and aggression. Everyone wants to be able to give and receive care and tenderness in a genuinely loving relationship.

All Futura Books are available at your bookshop or newsagent, or can be ordered from the following address:
Futura Books, Cash Sales Department,
P.O. Box 11, Falmouth, Cornwall.

Please send cheque or postal order (no currency), and allow 30p for postage and packing for the first book plus 15p for the second book and 12p for each additional book ordered up to a maximum charge of £1.29 in U.K.

Customers in Eire and B.F.P.O. please allow 30p for the first book, 15p for the second book plus 12p per copy for the next 7 books, thereafter 6p per book.

Overseas customers please allow 50p for postage and packing for the first book and 10p per copy for each additional book.